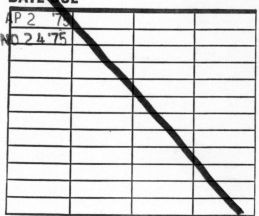

Problems in Prejudice

EUGENE HARTLEY

With a Foreword by

GARDNER MURPHY

1969

OCTAGON BOOKS

New York

Copyright 1946 by Eugene L. Hartley

Reprinted 1969
by special arrangement with Eugene L. Hartley

OCTAGON BOOKS
A DIVISION OF FARRAR, STRAUS & GIROUX, INC.
19 Union Square West
New York, N. Y. 10003

AM

LIBRARY OF CONGRESS CATALOG CARD NUMBER: 70-96197

Printed in U.S.A. by
TAYLOR PUBLISHING COMPANY
DALLAS, TEXAS

ıт IS A PLEASURE to be able to express publicly my deep appreciation of the guidance and encouragement given by Professors Robert S. Lynd, Ralph Linton, and Gardner Murphy who supervised the studies here reported. The financial gifts to Columbia University by the Pi Lambda Phi Foundation and the Conference on Jewish Relations made these studies possible. I regret that the need for anonymity of some of the institutions at which data were collected makes the full listing of co-operators inadvisable. I am none the less grateful to them for their help and for the contributions of the students who served as subjects.

Special mention should be made of the aid of Daniel Katz and John Gray Peatman who helped clarify some of the hypotheses developed here through discussions during the planning stages of these studies, as well as by securing the co-operation of students who served as subjects. Dr. Meyer Koch and the staff of the Essex Junior College in Newark, N.J., were very helpful in making possible some preliminary field work in exploring prejudice in a small college community. Dr. Martin Jenkins read an early version of this report and made cogent criticisms for which I am grateful, and Dr. Hyman Brandt critically reviewed some of the statistical discussions. Though I can include her name in this list of those to whom I am indebted, I cannot possibly adequately describe the contribution of Dr. Ruth E. Hartley who helped throughout the entire process of the development of these studies.

For permission to quote from previously published material, I am grateful to the Oxford University Press and the Office of Placement Service at Teachers College, Columbia University. Detailed references to authors and sources are given in the text.

E.L.H.

FOREWORD

THE VOLUME PRESENTED HERE, made possible by a grant to Columbia University from Pi Lamda Phi Foundation and the Conference on Jewish Relations, is characteristic of the trend towards the experimental and the quantitative in the study of social psychology.

Thirty years ago the realization began to spread that subgroups within a society do not "just naturally" develop friction and hostility; that differences of culture, religion and tradition do not inevitable prepare the soil for strife; that a great deal depends upon the outlook, the frame of reference, within which members of various sub-groups perceive each other; and that life histories and community studies may serve to show where friction reaches its maximum and where it is inconsequential or altogether lacking.

The biographical approach to individual prejudice, represented by Bruno Lasker's Race Attitudes in Children, paved the way for a more analytical inquiry. During the 1930's, as public-opinion research techniques developed, as interview data from church groups, trade unions, etc. became more refined and accurate, and as quantitative testing methods improved, it began to be possible to reveal not simply the gross amount of fear, prejudice, and hostility between sub-groups, but the roots from which such dispositions spring. It began to be more and more evident that it was ordinarily among the frightened, the confused and the sick that these reactions would be found in their highest intensity; that far from expressing normal self-interest, they were frequently self-defeating among the individuals professing the strongest antagonisms. One need only remember the very simple incident of the white trade-unionist who so often lost his job because of the importation of Negro strike breakers when the organization of Negroes within a common union would have been so simple. The "economic factor" is obvious; but it needs to be given a psychological formulation.

This element of irrationality, confusion, embitterment and

self-defeat began to be more and more transparent as the biographical materials were enriched by studies probing to a deeper level, namely by inclusion of psychiatric ways of thinking. Finally the idea began to emerge that there is a definite personality structure, a definite interrelation of traits that constitute a sort of core of the intolerant personality. At the same time it became clear that specific hostile patterns, such as feeling against the Negro, the Chinese, or the Jews are not psychological entities at all. They are manifestations of fear, particularly status fear, the dynamics of which show a very striking similarity regardless of the type of hostility involved. This means that there really is no such thing as Negro prejudice or anti-Semitism -- except as an expression of purely negative reality, like a vitamin deficiency. There is an acute absence of something, namely of the normal human interchange of ideas or feelings; there is a system of barriers. These barriers, however, are usually of the same general type and arise in about the same way regardless of the type of religious or racial hostility involved.

It was for this reason that Eugene Hartley, when asked in 1938 to give one year to the study of anti-Semitism, wisely insisted on viewing the problem more broadly, and on looking attentively and thoughtfully not at anti-Semitism as such, but at the tendency to irrational and confused separation of one's own group from that of other groups. Administering questionnaires to groups of college students, including groups of prospective teachers in teachers colleges, he undertook to find out what types of arbitrary rejection of social groups appeared, what kinds of human beings were excluded from the students' world of social participation. He found, as the text will show in detail, that the mechanisms by which any specific group, such as the Jewish group, is rejected by certain individuals in certain situations are mechanisms which run without essential change through the entire gamut of responses between groups. This is not to deny that for historical, religious or other reasons there may be qualitative differences between anti-Semitism and other types of prejudice. To deal, however, with first things first, it is of importance to note the very broad base of generality -- general rigidity and intolerance -- which serves as

primary source of all the specific phenomena in the prejudice
area. The first and major contribution of Hartley's thesis,
based upon data collected just before the war, is this generality of prejudice, a result better documented here than by any
other study yet published. It is true that many earlier studies
had showed the interrelation between various types of social
hostility. It remained, however, for this investigation to show
in quantitative form the degree of generality of the functions
involved, and in particular to show, by the introduction of
groups with fictitious names (against whom prejudice was as
high as it was against "real" groups) that we are dealing with
a true generality of pathological response, not with responses
based rationally on experience.

But the general trend needs to be seen as a function of individual personality. Upon the broad base of factors operating in
society at large are superimposed individual variations in personality patterns. Rigidity and hostility take different forms
in different people. Their implications for social living vary
with their context. For this reason the biographical studies
prepared here by Ruth Hartley are of value in showing the relation between formative factors in individual character and
the specific quality and quantity of prejudiced response. The
method as exhibited here has promise as an earnest of later
work with more material and more sustained clinical analysis.
The beginning, however, is of value and appropriately balances
the quantitative emphasis of the first part of the study.

Also of note is the inclusion here, for the first time in the
study of social attitudes, of William Stern's conception of
salience in personality structure. It is not true, Hartley
shows, that the amount of prejudice must necessarily be the
primary factor separating those who are openly anti-Semitic
from those who are not. Often of greater importance is the
question of the relation of the prejudice to the system of
values of the individual. One individual may have relatively
little prejudice but act on the basis of this prejudice when-
ever anything really vital comes his way. The trait stands at a
critical point in the structure of his life outlook. Another
individual may show ten times as much prejudice, may indeed express almost a menacing hostility to groups with whom he comes

in contact, and yet may have structured his life around certain other community values in such a way as to act consistently with restraint. Both reactions are dangerous, but there is a great deal of difference between the kinds of danger which they represent. Hartley succeeded in showing here by a very simple and objective method that salience and sheer quantity of response have different dimensions and that the student of prejudice must be prepared to deal with both.

This volume is then three studies in one: a major study of the generality of the prejudice reaction, and two minor studies dealing respectively with biographical data and with salience phenomena.

These studies would in normal course have appeared in the opening years of the 1940's. Dr. Hartley's war-time service has joined with production problems in delaying their appearance. But in a social order suffering from such dangerous malignancies as anti-Semitism, every such step towards clarification of its sources for most grateful recognition.

Gardner Murphy

CONTENTS

CHAPTER I

TOLERANCE OF COLLEGE STUDENTS

THE STUDIES IN THIS VOLUME are based on the behavior of college
students in test situations. They have meaning as a function of
the significance of the tests and the samples of students
studied. It was decided to limit the study to college students,
since they not only represent a population from which many of
the future leaders of social movements in our country will be
drawn, but one in many ways a significant sample of the general
community. Some of the findings will, of course, reflect only
the particular students who happen to have been studied. Other
findings, however, will represent generalizations which are
valid for college students in general and to a certain extent
for the nation (or even larger culture segments) which they
represent.

Distribution of Students

Samples were secured by arranging with teachers on the staffs
of several colleges. The teachers were personally known to the
writer, and the colleges were chosen partly on the basis of the
availability of such contacts. A more important criterion in
the selection of the schools was the desire to get an adequate
variety of institutions. It was recognized that it would be im-
possible, with the funds and time available, to define and lo-
cate the "typical" college. It seemed preferable to select
schools which differed widely, so that we might explore, not an
average, but to some extent the range of phenomena under investigation. By taking schools which varied, and making the analyses within each school separately, searching for common principles within successive samples, one might be more justified in
making generalizations than if one were to extend the analysis
of one or two schools which were supposed to be "typical."

Samples were secured from several liberal arts colleges; education majors in another college; two teacher training institu-

tions; and one collegiate school of business. Among these institutions, different philosophies of education were to be
found; students varied in vocational orientation, economic and
social backgrounds. There were members of discriminated-against
minorities and members of the dominant culture group. Both
sexes were represented. The colleges were:

Bennington
College of the City of New York - Arts
Columbia
Princeton
Howard University, College of Liberal Arts (Education majors)
"A" - a northeastern state-supported Teachers College
"B" - a state-supported Normal School in the same state
College of the City of New York - Business

The co-operating instructors were teachers of psychology or education who administered the questionnaires to their classes.
The sections selected were general, elementary classes in psychology and education chosen to satisfy the desire of the investigator to collect data from "representative" college students. When a class was selected for study, all the members of
the group were approached. Consequently, if there was any selection, it was on the basis of factors entering into the elec-
tion of courses in general psychology (and child or educational
psychology) at these schools, rather than in terms of the race
attitudes or ethnic interests of the students. In some of the
schools the course in which the data were collected was required for graduation, so that the students sampled in these
particular institutions were in all probability "fair samples"
of the college total. In the other institutions the courses
were prescribed only for students specializing in particular
fields or preparing for some particular future. Here, of course,
selection factors might be expected to operate. Table I gives a
description of the samples in each of the schools in terms of
sex of the respondents, and of their position in the school, as
the students described themselves.

   Since our interest in this study is primarily in terms of attitudes of the students towards a variety of ethnic groups, the
ethnic background of the individual students should be consid-

TABLE I

Description of the Samples Studied in Terms of Sex and School Year in Each School

	Male	Female	No Information	Total	Freshman	Sophomore	Junior	Senior	No Information
Bennington	0	31	0	31	20	8	3	0	0
College of the City of N.Y.--Arts	38	0	0	38	0	1	17	1	19
Columbia	136	0	0	136	1	63	51	1	20
Princeton	79	0	0	79	0	17	46	2	14
Howard	17	54	5	76	8	28	8	3	29
"A"--Teachers College	33	29	0	62	0	28	34	0	0
"B"--Normal School	59	0	7	66	0	48	3	0	15
College of the City of N.Y.--Business	107	21	0	128	4	22	17	3	82

ered. At the time the major data for the study were collected, the students were given an opportunity to indicate their own national and religious affiliations. In addition, they were asked to identify in similar fashion their fathers' and their mothers' affiliations (see Figure 1A). The frequency with which each national group, each religious group (and each of the listed political groups), were designated by the students as descriptive of themselves and of each of their parents was recorded. These designations were summated without regard to distinction between father and mother in order to give a single index of parental ethnic identification. Students frequently indicated affiliation with several national groups, in addition to American, and similarly attributed several affiliations to each parent. Undoubtedly some students tried to "kid" the test, but no correction for this was attempted. If the student said that his father was Irish and his mother Italian, a tally was made next to each of these two groups. If another student said that his mother was American but his father Irish, French, German, and Italian, five tallies would be made indicating the background of his parents, one for each of the groups mentioned rather than one for each parent. In Table II is presented a summary of the national groups most frequently referred to as self-descriptive and descriptive of parents in each of the schools. The frequency of the designation of each group is also indicated.

Students' Racial Attitudes

To serve as primary basis for study, it was necessary to get some indication of the students' attitude towards different ethnic groups. A slightly modified form of the social distance test, as originated by Bogardus (1) was decided upon, and attitudes toward each of forty-nine categories were elicited. Of these, thirty-five were ethnic groups, seven were religious groups, and seven were political groups (see Figure 1). The students indicated on an eight-point scale their reaction to each group, indicating to which of the following classifications members of the particular group might be admitted by them.

FIGURE I

NAME:_____CLASS:_____DATE:_____

DIRECTIONS. Below are the names of a number of groups of people. According
to your first feeling reaction to each of these groups of people (as a
group, and not the best or the worst members) encircle one or more of the
numbers following the name of the group to show the classifications to
which you would admit them. The numbers are to be interpreted:

        1. Would exclude from my country
        2. As visitors only to my country
        3. To citizenship in my country
        4. To employment in my occupation in my country

        5. To my school as classmates
        6. To my street as neighbors
        7. To my club as personal chums
        8. To close kinship by marriage

BE SURE TO ENTER A DESCRIPTION FOR EACH OF THE GROUPS LISTED.

1 Americans 1 2 3 4 5 6 7 8	26 Negro 1 2 3 4 5 6 7 8
2 American Indian 1 2 3 4 5 6 7 8	27 Pirenean 1 2 3 4 5 6 7 8
3 Arab 1 2 3 4 5 6 7 8	28 Polish 1 2 3 4 5 6 7 8
4 Argentine 1 2 3 4 5 6 7 8	29 Portuguese 1 2 3 4 5 6 7 8
5 Austrian 1 2 3 4 5 6 7 8	30 Rumanian 1 2 3 4 5 6 7 8
6 Canadian 1 2 3 4 5 6 7 8	31 Russian 1 2 3 4 5 6 7 8
7 French Canadian 1 2 3 4 5 6 7 8	32 Swedish 1 2 3 4 5 6 7 8
8 Chinese 1 2 3 4 5 6 7 8	33 Swiss 1 2 3 4 5 6 7 8
9 Czechoslovak 1 2 3 4 5 6 7 8	34 Turk 1 2 3 4 5 6 7 8
10 Danirean 1 2 3 4 5 6 7 8	35 Wallonian 1 2 3 4 5 6 7 8
11 Danish 1 2 3 4 5 6 7 8	36 Atheist 1 2 3 4 5 6 7 8
12 English 1 2 3 4 5 6 7 8	37 Fundamentalist 1 2 3 4 5 6 7
13 Filipino 1 2 3 4 5 6 7 8	38 Liberal Protestant 1 2 3 4 5 6 7 8
14 Finn 1 2 3 4 5 6 7 8	39 Roman Catholic 1 2 3 4 5 6 7 8
15 French 1 2 3 4 5 6 7 8	40 Russian Jew 1 2 3 4 5 6 7 8
	41 German Jew 1 2 3 4 5 6 7 8
16 German 1 2 3 4 5 6 7 8	42 American Jew 1 2 3 4 5 6 7
17 Greek 1 2 3 4 5 6 7 8	
18 Hindu 1 2 3 4 5 6 7 8	43 C I O Organizer 1 2 3 4 5 6 7 8
19 Hungarian 1 2 3 4 5 6 7 8	44 Communist 1 2 3 4 5 6 7 8
20 Irish 1 2 3 4 5 6 7 8	45 Fascist 1 2 3 4 5 6 7 8
	46 Labor Union Member 1 2 3 4 5 6 7 8
21 Italian 1 2 3 4 5 6 7 8	47 Nazi 1 2 3 4 5 6 7 8
22 Japanese 1 2 3 4 5 6 7 8	48 Political Refugee 1 2 3 4 5 6 7 8
23 Latvian 1 2 3 4 5 6 7 8	49 Socialist 1 2 3 4 5 6 7 8
24 Lithuanian 1 2 3 4 5 6 7 8	
25 Mexican 1 2 3 4 5 6 7 8	

If you would care to qualify any of the responses made above, or make additional statements, use the space below and the back of the page, if necessary.

FIGURE 1A

NAME:_____DATE:_____

In the list below, the various groups are preceded by the
letters I, F, M. Will you please go through the list carefully
and encircle the appropriate letters to show your background?
Before those groups of which you father is a member, draw a
circle around the F. Indicate the groups to which your mother
belongs by encircling the appropriate M's. Encircle the I before those groups to which you feel you belong. Remember that
any individual may belong to several of the groups listed. If
the listing is inadequate, will you please specify group mem-
berships in the space provided below.

I F M Americans	1 F M Negro	
I F M American Indian	I F M Pirenean	
I F M Arab	I F M Polish	
I F M Argentine	I F M Portuguese	
I F M Austrian	I F M Rumanian	
I F M Canadian	I F M Russian	
I F M French Canadian	I F M Swedish	
I F M Chinese	I F M Swiss	
I F M Czechoslovak	I F M Turk	
I F M Danirean	I F M Wallonian	
I F M Danish	I F M Atheist	
I F M English	I F M Fundamentalist	
I F M Filipino	I F M Liberal Protestant	
I F M Finn	I F M Roman Catholic	
I F M French	I F M Russian Jew	
	I F M German Jew	
I F M German	I F M American Jew	
I F M Greek		
I F M Hindu	I F M C I O Organizer	
I F M Hungarian	I F M Communist	
I F M Irish	I F M Fascist	
	I F M Labor Union Member	
I F M Italian	I F M Nazi	
I F M Japanese	I F M Political Refugee	
I F M Latvian	I F M Socialist	
I F M Lithuanian		
I F M Mexican		

For additions:
  I:_____
  F:_____
  M:_____

TABLE II

Students' Descriptions of Ethnic Backgrounds

"A"--Teachers College

National Background				Religious Background			
Self	No.	Parents	No.	Self	No.	Parents	No.
American	60	American	103	Roman Catholic	29	Roman Catholic	51
English	11	English	29	Liberal		Liberal	
Irish	10	Irish	22	Protestant*	11	Protestant	33
Italian	5	German	19	American Jew	11	American Jew	22
				Atheist*	5	Russian Jew	7

Bennington

National Background				Religious Background			
Self	No.	Parents	No.	Self	No.	Parents	No.
American	29	American	60	Liberal		Liberal	
English	5	English	20	Protestant	14	Protestant	42
French)		German	9	Atheist	6	Roman Catholic	3
German)		Irish	8	Fundamentalist*	2	American Jew	2
Irish)	1			Roman Catholic	2		
Italian)							
Negro)							

College of the City of N.Y.--Arts

National Background				Religious Background			
Self	No.	Parents	No.	Self	No.	Parents	No.
American	28	American	46	American Jew	18	American Jew	27
English	3	Russian	10	Atheist	5	Russian Jew	18
German	2	Polish	8	Liberal		Roman Catholic	4
Polish	2	Austrian	4	Protestant	3	Atheist	4
		Italian	4	Roman Catholic	3		

College of the City of N.Y.--Business

National Background				Religious Background			
Self	No.	Parents	No.	Self	No.	Parents	No.
American	114	American	136	American Jew	90	American Jew	122
English	4	Russian	53	Atheist	8	Russian Jew	82
Italian	4	Austrian	27	Roman Catholic	7	Roman Catholic	15
Polish	4	Polish	27	Russian Jew	5		
Russian	4	Rumanian	14				

TABLE II (Continued)

Columbia

National Background				Religious Background			
Self	No.	Parents	No.	Self	No.	Parents	No.
American	109	American	196	American Jew	40	American Jew	69
English	13	English	40	Liberal		Liberal	
Irish	11	German	28	Protestant	26	Protestant	57
German	6	Russian	21	Roman Catholic	19	Roman Catholic	45
French	5	Irish	20	Atheist	13		

Howard

National Background				Religious Background			
Self	No.	Parents	No.	Self	No.	Parents	No.
American		Negro	129	Liberal		Liberal	
Negro	63	American	116	Protestant	23	Protestant	41
American	53	American		Roman Catholic	3	Roman Catholic	11
American Indian	5	American Indian	21	American Jew	2		
French	3	English	10				
English)		French)	5				
Japanese)	2	Irish)					
Swiss)							

"B"--Normal School

National Background				Religious Background			
Self	No.	Parents	No.	Self	No.	Parents	No.
American	59	American	107	Liberal		Liberal	
English	16	English	38	Protestant	34	Protestant	69
Irish	9	German	24	Roman Catholic	12	Roman Catholic	22
German	8	Irish	24	American Jew	3	Fundamentalist	5
Swedish	2	French	8	Fundamentalist	2		
French	2						

Princeton

National Background				Religious Background			
Self	No.	Parents	No.	Self	No.	Parents	No.
American	76	American	153	Liberal		Liberal	
English	27	English	60	Protestant	41	Protestant	90
Irish	12	Irish	22	Roman Catholic	7	Roman Catholic	13
German	12	German	15	Atheist	7	Fundamentalist	11
French	5	French	12	Fundamentalist	2	American Jew	4

*Atheist and Fundamentalist were not defined in the original test sets.
Their inclusion in this Table refers to their use as such by the students.
"Liberal Protestant" has little meaning as a comparative term since owing to
an oversight in form construction, other opportunities for expressing background were omitted (see form illustrated in Fig. 1A).

1. Would exclude from my country
2. As visitors only to my country
3. To citizenship in my country
4. To employment in my occupation in my country
5. To my school as classmates
6. To my street as neighbors
7. To my club as personal chums
8. To close kinship by marriage

Analysis of the responses of the students on this scale indicated, as was expected, that it could only very roughly be considered a continuum. There were sufficiently frequent omissions, justified by marginal notes, to indicate that the students were giving careful consideration in their designations. For some students, for example, it was easier to admit members of a given group "to my school as classmates" than it was to admit them "to citizenship in my country." In spite of such irregularity, which tended to diminish the reliability of the indices developed, the highest point indicated in terms of nearness to the individual was used as the index of the tolerance of the respondent for the particular group, in spite of possible omissions at points lower in the scale. The scaling as conceived in this study was in the order given above, with the numerical indices 1-8 assigned as the numerical evaluation of each step in the scale. This involves the assumption of continuity, linearity, and the equivalence of the intervals between the statements. All of these assumptions are open to question, but will be accepted for the present and reconsidered to the extent that the data developed require review of the assumptions involved.

The tests were administered to the students by their own instructors, who attempted to establish an understanding and cooperative attitude. The students were assured that their responses would not redound to their personal disadvantage; that they would assist the research if they answered honestly. Every effort was made to convince the students of the desirability of sincere co-operation.

For the most part, the tests were given toward the end of 1938. The complete tabulation and the precise date of administration in each school is presented in the Appendix, Table A.

TABLE III

Tolerance for Each of the Forty-Nine Groups Toward Which Attitudes Were Expressed by Students at Each School as Indicated by the Median Response of Each Sample*

Item	Nationality	Princeton	"A"	"B"	C.C.N.Y.--Business
1	American	8.0	8.0	8.0	8.0
2	American Indian	5.3	6.9	7.2	7.1
3	Arab	2.8	2.8	2.5	4.0
4	Argentine	5.1	5.9	3.5	7.0
5	Austrian	6.4	6.9	3.3	7.7
6	Canadian	8.0	8.0	8.0	8.0
7	French Canadian	5.9	7.6	6.6	7.7
8	Chinese	2.7	5.1	2.4	3.7
9	Czechoslavak	4.5	5.6	2.9	7.5
10	Danirean	2.6	2.7	2.7	5.9
11	Danish	6.5	8.0	3.9	7.5
12	English	8.0	8.0	8.0	8.0
13	Filipino	2.8	3.3	3.4	5.2
14	Finn	5.9	7.2	4.6	7.3
15	French	6.6	8.0	6.2	8.0
16	German	6.8	7.8	4.7	7.6
17	Greek	2.9	6.2	3.1	6.3
18	Hindu	2.6	2.8	2.5	3.3
19	Hungarian	4.0	5.7	2.9	7.4
20	Irish	7.5	8.0	8.0	7.5
21	Italian	3.6	7.2	3.9	7.1
22	Japanese	2.3	2.8	2.1	2.7
23	Latvian	3.3	5.8	2.9	6.9
24	Lithuanian	3.0	5.8	2.8	7.1
25	Mexican	2.7	4.6	3.1	5.8
26	Negro	3.1	5.7	4.5	5.6
27	Pirenean	2.4	2.7	2.5	6.1
28	Polish	3.2	6.8	4.5	7.4
29	Portuguese	3.2	5.4	2.9	6.1
30	Rumanian	3.5	5.9	2.9	7.6
31	Russian	3.3	5.8	3.3	7.7
32	Swedish	7.3	7.9	6.4	7.5
33	Swiss	7.3	8.0	6.7	7.7
34	Turk	2.7	2.9	2.4	5.1
35	Wallonian	2.8	2.9	2.4	5.5
36	Atheist	7.2	3.4	1.9	7.2
37	Fundamentalist	7.0	6.5	3.8	7.3
38	Liberal Protestant	8.0	8.0	8.0	7.4
39	Roman Catholic	7.1	8.0	7.8	7.4
40	Russian Jew	2.8	6.6	3.3	8.0
41	German Jew	2.9	6.8	3.8	8.0
42	American Jew	3.6	7.2	5.6	8.0
43	C.I.O. Organizer	3.7	3.9	3.9	7.9
44	Communist	2.1	2.1	1.8	5.8
45	Fascist	2.0	2.2	1.8	1.8
46	Labor Union Member	5.0	7.7	6.4	8.0
47	Nazi	1.97	1.9	1.8	1.8
48	Political Refugee	3.7	5.4	2.8	8.0
49	Socialist	5.0	4.0	2.8	7.9

*The numbers are to be interpreted:
1. Would exclude from my country
2. As visitors only to my country
3. To citizenship in my country
4. To employment in my occupation in my country

5. To my school as classmates
6. To my street as neighbors
7. To my club as personal chums
8. To close kinship by marriage

Item	Nationality	Columbia	Bennington	Howard	C.C.N.Y.--Arts
1	American	8.0	8.0	5.9	8.0
2	American Indian	6.2	5.5	3.9	6.6
3	Arab	3.4	4.2	2.8	3.8
4	Argentine	5.7	5.7	2.8	6.7
5	Austrian	6.7	7.3	2.9	7.0
6	Canadian	8.0	8.0	3.9	7.4
7	French Canadian	7.1	6.5	3.7	7.2
8	Chinese	3.9	5.1	2.6	5.3
9	Czechoslavak	5.9	6.8	2.8	7.0
10	Danirean	2.2	4.0	2.6	3.6
11	Danish	7.0	8.0	2.9	7.0
12	English	8.0	8.0	3.9	7.8
13	Filipino	3.5	5.2	3.4	4.0
14	Finn	6.6	6.6	2.8	7.3
15	French	7.7	8.0	3.9	7.3
16	German	6.9	8.0	2.1	7.6
17	Greek	5.3	5.8	1.1	6.8
18	Hindu	2.9	5.6	2.6	5.4
19	Hungarian	4.9	6.4	2.7	6.8
20	Irish	7.4	7.6	3.6	7.6
21	Italian	5.9	6.6	2.7	7.1
22	Japanese	2.7	3.9	2.3	3.6
23	Latvian	3.8	6.2	2.6	6.3
24	Lithuanian	4.6	6.2	2.7	6.6
25	Mexican	3.4	5.4	3.3	5.7
26	Negro	5.1	5.4	8.0	5.5
27	Pirenean	2.3	5.3	2.5	3.4
28	Polish	4.5	6.2	2.7	7.0
29	Portuguese	3.7	5.8	2.7	7.0
30	Rumanian	4.7	6.2	2.7	7.0
31	Russian	5.1	7.0	2.9	6.8
32	Swedish	6.8	7.6	3.2	7.3
33	Swiss	7.2	8.0	3.2	7.2
34	Turk	3.4	5.5	2.5	5.0
35	Wallonian	2.1	5.0	2.5	3.3
36	Atheist	7.0	8.0	2.1	7.0
37	Fundamentalist	6.5	8.0	2.9	6.3
38	Liberal Protestant	7.6	8.0	3.9	7.4
39	Roman Catholic	7.3	7.6	3.2	7.3
40	Russian Jew	5.6	6.4	2.7	8.0
41	German Jew	6.1	6.6	2.5	8.0
42	American Jew	7.4	6.4	3.7	8.0
43	C.I.O. Organizer	4.6	7.4	3.8	7.5
44	Communist	3.2	7.6	1.1	6.3
45	Fascist	1.9	6.2	1.7	1.9
46	Labor Union Member	6.95	7.6	4.3	7.6
47	Nazi	1.8	3.0	1.6	1.7
48	Political Refugee	5.4	7.6	2.2	7.5
49	Socialist	6.0	7.95	2.8	7.3

*The numbers are to be interpreted:
1. Would exclude from my country
2. As visitors only to my country
3. To citizenship in my country
4. To employment in my occupation in my country

5. To my school as classmates
6. To my street as neighbors
7. To my club as personal chums
8. To close kinship by marriage

It is to be noted that expression of attitude was elicited
from the students at Princeton after the disappearance of Aus-
tria as an independent nation and during a period when the
roles of England, France, and Czechoslovakia in world affairs
and in world thinking were undergoing radical revision.

In some of the schools signatures on the papers were required
as a matter of course. In other schools students were given the
option of signing or not signing. When such option was given,
it was ordinarily presented in a form such as to discourage
signing the name. Since the fact of signing one's name to an
attitude test might tend to influence the degree of tolerance
expressed, it is not fair to compare directly the tolerance of
students who did not sign their names with that of students who
did submit signed attitude expressions.

The median attitude toward each group at each school is presented in Table III. The medians were computed assuming continuity of each step from the digit up to, but not including, the
next unit. Thus a score of three was interpreted to indicate
that the respondent would admit the members of the particular
group to citizenship in the United States and possibly all suc-
ceeding evidences of tolerance up to but not including admission to employment in the student's occupation in this country.
The table shows that at the "A" - Teachers' College, for example, the median attitude of tolerance for Arabs, listed in the
table, is 2.8; this means that by and large Arabs would be admitted as visitors to this country and almost admitted to the
point of citizenship. People from the Argentine, toward whom
the median attitude of these students is represented in the
table by 5.9, would be admitted to school as classmates of the
respondents and almost admitted to residence on their streets
as neighbors.

A more complete presentation of the distribution of the responses of students at each school to each item appears in Table IV. Here, expressed in percentages, is the number of students who indicated each item in the scale as the most intimate
relationship to which they would admit each group.

It seemed desirable to have some way of establishing a hierarchy of the preferences expressed for the various ethnic and
national groups. To this end an index was computed representing

TABLE IV

Frequency Distribution (in Percent) of the Limits of Social Nearness Designated for Each Group by the Samples in Each School*

Item	"B"--Normal School								C.C.N.Y.--Arts							
	1	2	3	4	5	6	7	8	1	2	3	4	5	6	7	8
1	0	0	14	5	0	2	6	74	0	0	17	0	0	9	11	63
2	0	0	16	9	7	13	30	25	0	6	23	3	9	14	29	17
3	25	48	2	3	3	2	12	6	14	23	14	3	6	3	23	14
4	11	34	11	8	3	8	14	12	0	17	17	3	3	11	17	31
5	9	38	9	7	5	9	5	17	0	9	21	3	3	12	18	33
6	3	5	12	3	3	12	9	53	0	9	20	0	0	11	20	40
7	3	19	16	0	3	14	11	54	0	14	14	3	3	11	17	37
8	33	44	2	2	3	8	9	0	6	31	6	3	11	6	20	17
9	11	41	12	2	8	6	6	14	0	11	17	3	0	17	14	37
10	21	42	15	4	4	2	4	9	12	24	20	4	4	4	16	16
11	3	30	18	5	5	6	11	23	0	14	17	0	0	17	14	37
12	3	5	15	2	3	3	5	64	0	3	20	3	0	11	14	49
13	9	32	22	5	6	6	14	6	3	26	20	3	9	6	23	11
14	6	29	12	5	8	8	9	24	0	11	17	0	3	11	20	37
15	3	16	16	6	8	6	11	33	0	6	20	0	6	14	9	46
16	12	21	15	3	5	0	12	32	11	6	14	0	0	11	9	49
17	8	41	14	3	6	12	8	9	0	17	14	3	3	14	26	23
18	23	58	6	1	1	1	8	1	12	21	9	3	15	6	21	15
19	11	42	17	5	2	5	6	14	3	17	14	3	0	14	17	20
20	0	10	16	3	3	8	10	50	0	6	14	3	3	11	20	43
21	14	28	9	3	6	6	11	23	6	6	11	6	3	14	23	31
22	45	36	2	3	2	3	9	2	17	26	9	6	9	3	20	11
23	14	41	16	3	3	5	8	10	0	26	14	3	3	11	14	29
24	19	38	11	3	2	7	6	14	0	21	15	3	3	15	15	29
25	14	35	15	5	5	9	8	9	6	20	11	6	9	9	14	26
26	9	17	18	11	14	9	20	3	6	12	24	0	18	15	15	12
27	24	54	9	0	0	4	7	2	13	29	21	4	0	4	17	12
28	9	26	11	9	3	6	15	21	6	15	12	0	6	9	18	33
29	9	42	16	5	3	6	11	8	3	21	12	3	6	6	26	24
30	9	42	14	3	3	6	11	12	3	21	12	0	6	9	15	35
31	15	30	15	5	6	5	8	17	6	15	15	0	3	15	12	35
32	5	16	16	3	3	16	5	38	0	9	18	3	0	15	12	42
33	5	14	15	6	2	11	5	43	0	3	29	0	0	15	15	38
34	26	54	3	2	2	3	6	5	9	24	15	3	12	3	24	12
35	31	48	8	2	4	2	2	4	17	25	25	4	4	4	4	17
36	51	14	6	3	2	5	6	14	12	9	18	0	9	3	12	38
37	10	25	19	6	8	4	10	19	7	10	24	0	3	10	10	34
38	2	3	6	2	5	5	12	65	0	0	30	0	0	12	15	42
39	0	5	8	2	2	8	30	46	0	0	30	0	0	12	21	36
40	20	21	14	3	8	11	17	8	3	3	24	0	0	12	6	53
41	17	24	12	5	9	11	17	6	3	3	20	0	0	9	6	53
42	12	11	15	5	12	9	21	15	3	0	24	0	0	6	0	68
43	26	10	15	13	7	7	2	21	3	3	26	3	0	9	12	44
44	65	18	6	3	0	2	3	3	18	18	12	0	0	9	12	32
45	62	25	8	0	0	2	3	2	59	9	9	0	6	6	3	9
46	3	8	16	16	2	8	6	38	3	0	24	3	3	6	15	45
47	62	20	6	0	5	2	0	6	68	9	3	0	9	6	0	6
48	22	35	7	3	2	5	3	23	3	3	26	0	0	9	18	41
49	34	20	17	3	2	0	3	20	9	6	26	0	0	3	18	38

*The numbers are to be interpreted:
1. Would exclude from my country
2. As visitors only to my country
3. To citizenship in my country
4. To employment in my occupation in my country
5. To my school as classmates
6. To my street as neighbors
7. To my club as personal chums
8. To close kinship by marriage

TABLE IV (Continued)

Item	"A"--Teachers College								Bennington							
	1	2	3	4	5	6	7	8	1	2	3	4	5	6	7	8
1	2	0	5	3	2	3	5	81	0	0	0	0	3	6	3	87
2	2	0	19	3	13	15	39	10	0	3	23	10	27	13	17	7
3	15	41	8	0	8	13	11	3	0	23	23	13	13	10	16	3
4	3	26	11	0	11	11	16	20	0	16	10	10	13	19	6	26
5	7	11	16	3	7	7	20	28	3	3	6	0	13	19	10	39
6	0	5	8	3	3	6	10	65	0	0	3	0	13	10	0	74
7	0	13	16	2	2	8	16	43	0	13	6	0	19	19	10	35
8	18	28	3	0	15	7	28	2	6	29	10	0	23	13	13	6
9	7	18	10	5	16	10	11	23	0	13	13	3	6	15	13	35
10	28	33	8	0	8	8	5	10	5	32	11	5	5	16	21	5
11	3	8	11	2	5	3	16	51	0	3	3	0	6	19	13	55
12	0	5	5	2	2	7	11	69	0	0	0	0	6	3	3	87
13	8	40	7	5	7	7	20	5	0	33	10	3	17	13	20	3
14	0	14	10	5	8	8	22	32	0	14	10	4	7	21	10	34
15	0	8	10	0	3	7	22	49	3	0	3	0	3	10	20	60
16	13	10	7	0	2	7	15	47	0	0	3	6	10	10	6	64
17	5	25	8	3	8	7	27	15	0	19	10	6	16	16	16	16
18	15	44	2	2	8	8	20	0	0	26	10	3	16	19	13	13
19	7	19	12	7	7	8	17	24	0	19	16	3	6	23	6	32
20	0	7	8	2	2	8	13	61	0	6	10	10	3	13	10	48
21	7	15	10	3	2	7	25	32	3	6	6	3	16	19	13	32
22	25	33	5	2	10	8	15	0	10	29	10	0	13	19	13	6
23	3	29	9	2	9	9	16	24	3	21	6	0	14	21	21	14
24	2	24	14	2	10	8	15	25	3	27	3	3	10	17	17	20
25	7	35	5	5	8	8	22	10	10	17	10	7	17	17	10	13
26	3	8	15	5	27	15	23	2	0	6	26	3	35	10	16	3
27	23	39	5	2	7	11	7	5	4	29	8	4	17	8	21	8
28	2	13	16	3	10	8	20	28	0	10	10	10	16	16	10	29
29	10	23	8	3	15	8	20	12	0	16	10	10	16	16	10	23
30	7	20	7	2	15	12	8	29	0	20	10	3	13	20	10	23
31	5	23	9	2	14	9	14	25	0	3	6	13	10	16	16	35
32	0	8	8	3	5	10	18	47	0	0	13	6	6	16	10	48
33	0	5	7	2	5	10	22	50	0	0	10	3	3	13	10	61
34	15	40	2	0	10	10	15	7	0	32	3	3	19	19	16	6
35	27	25	14	2	5	11	7	9	5	26	11	5	21	11	5	11
36	36	12	5	3	3	8	10	22	0	0	3	3	3	13	23	55
37	11	17	15	0	4	6	19	28	0	7	0	0	7	13	17	57
38	0	3	9	0	3	5	25	54	0	3	3	0	3	6	6	77
39	2	0	9	0	3	7	28	52	0	0	6	0	10	13	32	39
40	12	11	14	0	9	7	26	21	0	13	6	0	19	23	26	13
41	11	9	15	7	5	5	27	20	0	13	6	3	13	23	26	16
42	10	2	14	7	5	7	29	26	6	6	6	0	16	29	16	19
43	18	14	21	3	7	7	9	21	3	6	13	0	6	13	16	42
44	49	15	7	5	3	2	8	12	13	6	6	0	3	6	23	42
45	46	25	7	2	2	7	3	8	20	10	10	0	6	20	16	20
46	4	5	11	12	5	7	9	46	3	0	13	3	10	10	16	45
47	56	20	3	0	3	5	5	7	32	16	10	0	3	13	13	13
48	14	18	12	3	7	7	14	25	3	13	6	0	10	6	16	45
49	24	9	17	3	3	2	14	28	3	0	6	0	16	10	13	51

*The numbers are to be interpreted:
1. Would exclude from my country
2. As visitors only to my country
3. To citizenship in my country
4. To employment in my occupation in my country
5. To my school as classmates
6. To my street as neighbors
7. To my club as personal chums
8. To close kinship by marriage

TABLE IV (Continued)

Item	Princeton								Howard							
	1	2	3	4	5	6	7	8	1	2	3	4	5	6	7	8
1	4	0	6	1	0	0	0	88	3	4	36	3	5	7	4	38
2	1	4	30	11	9	14	24	5	3	10	41	6	10	6	10	13
3	16	43	9	4	4	7	17	1	21	51	13	0	7	3	1	4
4	3	27	8	12	9	12	20	11	6	51	18	8	4	7	3	3
5	3	18	8	8	9	14	13	28	9	49	18	7	6	6	1	3
6	0	4	4	3	1	3	9	77	7	18	27	6	8	17	1	15
7	1	21	9	6	14	19	.12	18	4	26	28	4	7	14	3	13
8	23	41	9	1	6	3	17	0	28	40	10	3	7	7	3	3
9	5	23	18	8	5	12	10	19	13	45	21	6	7	4	3	1
10	29	31	4	10	4	6	6	10	16	55	11	5	3	6	2	3
11	4	10	13	9	9	14	9	34	7	43	21	7	11	6	1	3
12	1	0	5	3	0	4	5	82	6	8	36	6	10	10	6	19
13	16	43	8	4	4	10	16	0	14	26	22	10	10	4	1	13
14	0	14	16	12	9	16	14	19	12	49	13	4	13	4	3	1
15	1	14	14	4	5	19	9	33	3	14	38	3	8	11	7	15
16	8	10	10	9	5	8	10	39	49	22	11	4	4	5	3	3
17	12	42	13	3	6	8	10	6	20	43	16	9	6	4	1	1
18	18	49	5	5	1	4	16	1	23	46	11	3	7	1	3	6
19	6	31	12	8	5	10	14	13	17	47	13	7	6	4	4	1
20	0	12	6	8	9	6	14	44	10	22	30	10	12	7	6	3
21	14	31	6	9	5	10	9	14	31	27	25	1	3	6	4	3
22	38	36	4	3	5	3	12	0	38	42	11	1	3	1	1	3
23	7	38	12	8	5	8	11	10	18	52	15	4	4	3	1	1
24	7	42	11	7	5	7	11	11	18	48	20	5	5	2	2	2
25	22	41	8	4	6	6	9	4	8	38	15	15	7	4	3	8
26	29	18	21	11	11	4	7	0	0	0	18	5	1	3	1	72
27	28	52	6	4	4	2	0	4	28	48	11	6	3	2	2	2
28	9	38	16	4	6	9	6	12	18	46	20	8	3	1	1	1
29	8	39	13	11	12	4	8	6	16	50	11	7	3	4	1	7
30	8	33	14	8	7	9	8	11	9	58	16	7	4	1	1	3
31	12	34	13	4	5	8	9	16	13	43	19	4	8	6	3	4
32	3	14	8	8	5	6	19	36	6	38	29	8	8	7	3	1
33	0	8	13	8	5	12	16	39	6	38	28	7	8	6	4	3
34	22	42	6	6	5	5	10	3	24	47	13	6	3	3	1	3
35	25	32	7	9	7	2	9	11	25	55	8	7	2	2	0	2
36	16	6	8	5	5	6	17	36	46	28	6	4	3	6	3	4
37	7	10	12	6	7	6	15	36	18	39	16	8	8	6	2	3
38	3	1	7	1	4	4	9	71	6	15	33	5	8	8	8	18
39	5	4	10	0	5	13	17	45	6	19	30	1	9	9	6	20
40	34	22	8	4	11	7	9	5	16	50	17	3	6	3	2	3
41	29	22	9	4	8	10	13	5	27	44	16	0	5	5	2	3
42	25	12	19	5	11	8	13	7	13	11	37	11	11	7	2	6
43	30	6	19	5	4	4	8	23	13	19	21	25	3	5	5	10
44	48	13	6	3	3	4	6	17	52	20	11	3	2	3	5	10
45	49	14	4	1	4	6	8	13	76	14	6	0	0	2	2	2
46	9	5	26	9	5	12	6	27	6	14	22	28	6	8	5	12
47	51	16	3	0	4	8	9	10	85	6	3	0	2	0	2	2
48	21	19	13	3	7	7	8	23	44	30	13	3	2	3	2	3
49	22	13	12	2	6	4	12	29	28	27	17	3	3	7	3	12

*The numbers are to be interpreted:
1. Would exclude from my country
2. As visitors only to my country
3. To citizenship in my country
4. To employment in my occupation in my country
5. To my school as classmates
6. To my street as neighbors
7. To my club as personal chums
8. To close kinship by marriage

TABLE IV (Continued)

Item	Columbia								C.C.N.Y.--Business							
	1	2	3	4	5	6	7	8	1	2	3	4	5	6	7	8
1	3	0	7	1	2	5	4	77	0	0	0	0	1	2	7	90
2	2	1	23	3	16	15	31	10	0	1	11	4	17	14	34	19
3	10	34	9	1	13	10	14	8	8	40	1	3	14	6	18	11
4	2	23	7	6	14	12	19	17	1	13	11	3	8	15	24	26
5	6	14	11	3	5	12	19	30	2	9	5	4	6	15	16	44
6	1	2	9	5	1	8	13	61	0	0	1	2	2	9	24	60
7	2	12	10	5	10	8	20	34	0	6	1	2	6	14	32	40
8	13	29	5	4	17	6	23	3	15	32	5	2	15	10	16	5
9	5	16	15	4	8	14	18	19	1	5	10	2	8	12	26	36
10	18	29	10	5	10	9	15	5	2	32	5	0	13	12	18	18
11	1	7	17	4	8	11	19	35	0	6	3	3	5	20	28	35
12	1	2	10	2	1	8	14	63	0	1	2	1	2	6	25	64
13	5	33	19	2	14	10	17	1	5	32	6	4	16	12	18	7
14	1	8	13	5	9	23	22	21	0	6	6	3	8	16	31	30
15	2	7	12	5	5	7	18	46	0	2	2	2	3	12	27	52
16	8	11	8	4	11	8	16	35	7	7	3	2	8	10	20	42
17	8	17	15	4	15	13	17	12	1	20	8	1	18	11	24	19
18	13	37	7	1	12	10	17	3	11	37	5	2	13	10	15	6
19	6	18	14	6	9	12	16	18	1	10	6	2	9	13	23	36
20	2	5	9	2	6	13	23	40	0	2	1	1	12	14	41	28
21	7	10	14	4	13	11	20	21	3	13	6	0	14	11	30	23
22	25	31	5	1	16	6	14	2	30	29	5	0	14	6	14	4
23	7	22	18	1	11	14	15	13	1	18	5	1	14	13	20	29
24	7	21	16	3	12	11	16	16	1	13	7	1	13	13	24	28
25	10	32	12	4	14	9	10	10	4	25	9	1	15	13	20	13
26	13	7	21	4	28	7	17	2	5	5	15	2	36	12	22	4
27	15	34	14	3	11	4	10	7	4	20	8	1	16	12	21	17
28	5	22	12	9	11	13	14	12	0	10	7	2	11	12	19	38
29	6	27	17	5	12	12	12	10	3	17	6	2	19	18	16	19
30	5	19	15	6	10	17	17	12	0	10	6	2	8	15	19	42
31	14	16	8	6	11	12	14	20	0	9	4	3	5	17	22	42
32	2	5	14	2	9	15	18	35	0	2	5	2	9	17	33	34
33	3	3	10	2	7	15	24	36	0	3	6	1	6	13	30	41
34	10	28	16	3	15	10	12	7	4	39	6	1	15	6	18	12
35	16	31	12	3	10	8	10	8	5	28	5	2	23	5	18	15
36	9	6	12	3	8	6	15	41	10	8	8	2	11	8	21	33
37	6	10	19	1	8	12	21	24	1	16	9	2	7	6	26	31
38	1	1	12	2	5	12	30	37	0	2	5	2	7	15	44	25
39	2	2	15	1	5	17	28	31	0	0	4	3	10	15	41	27
40	16	11	11	3	12	5	14	28	0	2	2	2	3	7	12	72
41	14	9	11	4	11	7	14	31	0	2	2	1	2	9	14	71
42	20	3	11	2	7	7	20	31	0	1	0	0	2	3	6	89
43	26	8	14	3	6	10	13	20	5	4	8	1	6	12	16	48
44	37	11	8	1	6	12	10	16	28	13	5	0	5	11	15	23
45	56	13	10	1	5	10	16	34	60	21	2	0	4	4	2	7
46	5	7	22	4	3	10	16	34	0	2	6	2	1	7	14	67
47	65	15	7	3	1	4	4	2	66	17	4	0	1	3	3	5
48	13	17	16	2	4	9	12	27	2	4	2	2	2	11	19	56
49	14	14	15	3	4	6	18	26	4	10	3	2	7	12	14	49

*The numbers are to be interpreted:
1. Would exclude from my country
2. As visitors only to my country
3. To citizenship in my country
4. To employment in my occupation in my country

5. To my school as classmates
6. To my street as neighbors
7. To my club as personal chums
8. To close kinship by marriage

the number of students within the sample whose upper limit of tolerance for any particular group was less than admission to citizenship in this country. This index derived from the number of students whose tolerance score for the particular group was either one or two. The frequency differed for each of the national groups included in the attitude test and the rankings assigned were unequivocal, as can be established by study of Table IV. The thirty-five ethnic groups included in this part of the test were ranked in order of preference on the basis of this index of exclusion from citizenship and also on the basis of the median attitude as listed in Table IV. The two series of rankings (for each school separately) were correlated by the rank-difference method of correlation. The coefficients so computed were as follows:

Princeton	.98	C.C.N.Y.--Business	.82
Columbia	.90	Howard	.92
Bennington	.84	"A"	.91
C.C.N.Y.--Arts	.85	"B"	.98

These coefficients are all sufficiently high to indicate that the rankings assigned by the method used in our analysis (the percentage excluding from citizenship) are quite similar to the median score patterns.

As might be expected, we find in the above analyses evidence that the students are reacting differently to the different national groups included in our test. Students are differentiating on the basis of nationality. They do not respond the same to English and Japanese, French and Turk, Swede and Chinese. We notice, too, that the students in the different schools seem to be responding differently. At Howard the Negro ranks high on the list, though he ranks low elsewhere. City College students are much more tolerant of German Jews than are the students at "B." Princeton students display toward C.I.O. Organizers far more antagonism than do the students at Bennington. Among the thirty-five groups studied in terms of the tendency of the students to desire the members of these particular groups to be excluded from citizenship, we find that the number of groups excluded by 50 percent or more of the sample at each college varies greatly. Bennington students do not offer a majority

vote for the exclusion of even one of the thirty-five. "B"
would exclude fourteen of the thirty-five; and at Howard, twen-
ty-two would be excluded by at least 50 percent of the sample.
Some of these differences may be due to the factors associated
with the differences between signed and unsigned expressions
of attitude, but there is enough difference between "A" and
Howard, for example, to warrant our conclusion. A third point
is also obvious. Different individuals within each sample differ with respect to the attitude they expressed toward any one
group. The frequency distribution presented in Table IV shows
their variability quite clearly. Some students would want Germans and Turks excluded from the country; others say they would
be willing to admit them to close kinship by marriage.

General Considerations

Before proceeding with a more intensive study, let us review
some general considerations. Why do we make an effort to study
students' attitudes towards national and racial groups? An interest in the study of student attitudes means an interest in
the rules governing the behavior of these students. If we know
their attitudes, presumably we know the rules in accordance
with which they are behaving, and are therefore in a position
to predict their behavior. In the search for these rules, at
least three approaches are made. (1) Sometimes the investigator
assumes that the responding individual is aware of the background of his behavior and knows what is involved in different
types of situations. Interviews and questionnaires have been
utilized to study people's attitudes. At times they have been
used to try to get people to say just what their attitudes are,
what the rules governing their behavior might be. Experience
has demonstrated that this approach yields material which may
be of interest but which does not give an adequate basis for
prediction of behavior. The statement of the rules themselves
seems to be a form of behavior rather than a formulation of the
basic principles governing behavior.

(2) A second approach is tried in studies which undertake to
present verbally a series of situations in order to get responses from which the rules governing behavior might be in-

ferred. Some of these studies have implied that the responses made to a verbally described situation have predictive value for behavior in a "real" representation of the same situation. Careful analysis suggests that this is not inevitably true.

(3) Still a third approach has been made. The questionnaires may be used to give individuals an opportunity to display behavior of the sort in which we are interested. This behavior may then be analyzed to give information concerning the rules governing behavior of the sort in which we are interested, in one type of situation (the test situation). Research is needed, of course, to discover whether the same rules obtain in other types of situations. The questionnaire approach has been used in this study for the last mentioned purpose. It represents an experimentally controlled situation in which the individual can behave, and the laws governing his behavior in this sample situation may be found to apply in other types of situations.

The questionnaires used in this study are conceived as forms for eliciting behavior in standardized conditions, so that we may compare the responses of different individuals. If, in our questionnaire, one individual responds more favorably toward a given group than does another, our interpretation is simply that, in this situation, Individual A has responded more favorably toward the group than has Individual B. If we can learn more about the reason for the differences between A and B, we shall be satisfied that we are contributing to an understanding of human behavior. It is an open question whether the explanation offered for the interpretation of the differences between A and B under these conditions are the same as would explain their possible differences under other circumstances. Presumably, if we can elucidate the dynamics of discriminatory behavior, we can improve understanding of other situations.

With this orientation towards the significance of a questionnaire study, let us attempt to repeat the summary given above of preliminary consideration of the behaviors of the students in the several colleges. (1) The students react differently to the different groups. That is, they display tendencies to discriminate among races, nations, and religious groups. (2) The groups at the different colleges react differently to the various national and racial stimuli used in the test situation.

(3) Individuals within each group differ in their responses. If we set these three major observations as problems to be studied and explained, we may make a start in our understanding of similar observations made under other forms of test or life conditions. In the following pages, we shall report the efforts made to analyze items one and three. We shall also attempt to define an attitude variable which is important to consider in general discussions of race problems. This variable, attitude "salience," is subjected to some preliminary study and results are presented.

CHAPTER II

ANALYSIS OF TOLERANCE

A Pattern of Preferences

IN THE PRECEDING CHAPTER evidence was presented of a differential preference expressed by the students for the various groups included in our attitude test. For the present, let us concern ourself with the attitudes toward the thirty-five racial and national groups (omitting the religious and political groups). Thirty-two of these thirty-five groups are readily recognized. Three of them, the Danireans, Pireneans, and Wallonians, are fairly novel and will be discussed below. In the ranking of preference for these ethnic groups in terms of the expressed tolerance of the students at the different schools, certain sequences seem similar. To describe this similarity in more quantitative form coefficients of rank-difference correlation were computed for the rankings of the groups at each college. These coefficients, presented in Table V, range from .69 to .97. In spite of the difference in the backgrounds of the students, differences in experience and national and racial stock, they seem to have basically the same pattern of preferences. This pattern of liking Canadians and the English best, and liking Hindus and Turks least, seems to be a common American orientation. That this pattern is a significant part of the general American cultural scheme seems to be demonstrated by the correlation between the preferences shown by one of the eight groups studied and the pattern of preference expressed by the cross section of the American population presented by Bogardus in 1928 in Immigration and Race Attitudes (2). This volume presents the responses of 1725 American representing a general cross section of the country, to forty different nations and races. Bogardus' listing of forty was compared with the list used in this study. Twenty-six of the groups appeared on both lists. The percent of the samples in 1928 and one of the college groups ("B") in 1938 which would deny the groups

TABLE V

Coefficients of Rank-Difference Correlation of Patterns of Preference for Thirty-Five Nations and Races Displayed by Students at the Different Schools

	Bennington	Columbia	C.C.N.Y. Arts	C.C.N.Y. Business	Howard	"A"	"B"	Princeton
Bennington		.88	.87	.87	.69	.89	.86	.88
Columbia	.88		.95	.92	.77	.97	.92	.95
C.C.N.Y.-- Arts	.87	.95		.90	.79	.93	.89	.92
C.C.N.Y.-- Business	.87	.92	.90		.78	.94	.88	.92
Howard	.69	.77	.79	.78		.79	.86	.68
"A"	.89	.97	.93	.94	.79		.92	.92
"B"	.86	.92	.89	.88	.86	.92		.87
Princeton	.88	.95	.92	.92	.68	.92	.87	

citizenship ("exclude from the country," and "admit to the
country as visitors only," combined), are shown in Table VI.
Rank difference correlation between the two lists gives rho=.78.
This coefficient demonstrates a highly significant relationship
between the two patterns of preference. The students are responding in the pattern generally prevalent a decade earlier.
In sheer amount there appears to be a consistent difference in
tolerance; the collegians in 1938 were less tolerant than the
more widely selected group in 1928. However, this particular
college sample was arbitrarily selected and the level of tolerance displayed by these students cannot be considered as representative for college students in general. The college sample
used in this demonstration of the relationship between the con-
temporary pattern and that a decade earlier was group B whose
pattern correlated substantially with those of the other schools
(rho varies between .86 and .92).

There is much evidence available in the literature to confirm
our suggestion that this pattern of preference is practically an
American institution. We find in the present material evidence
that the girls at Bennington, in Vermont, display the same pattern as the Negro students at Howard University in Washington,
D.C. Guilford in 1931 reported on the preferences of students
in seven different colleges across the country from Florida to
Washington, and found that similarity of the patterns of preference for the fifteen groups used in the test could be described
by correlation coefficients ranging from .84 to .99 (5). Meltzer,
studying attitudes of school children in St. Louis, found preferences very similar to those expressed by college students. He
found that in these children the patterns were very similar
among Jews and Catholics and Protestants when studied separately,
among the Negroes and Whites, rural and urban, and among the
children from the different economic levels (9). Let us accept,
then, the conclusion that there is a standardized pattern of
preferences or prejudices prevalent in the United States.

The Generalized Nature of Tolerance

In the preceding chapter attention has been called to the
differences in the general level of tolerance at the different

TABLE VI

Comparison of Pattern of Preference of One Group of College
Students in 1938 with a General Cross Section of the Coun-
try as Reported in 1928. Percent of Students at "B"
Unwilling to Admit Each Group to Citizenship and
Comparable Index from Bogardus' Tabulations

Nationality	College Sample 1938	Bogardus' Cross Section 1928
Americans	0	1.2
American Indian	0	9.3
Canadian	8	2.0
French Canadian	22	5.2
Chinese	77	67.6
Czechoslovak	52	35.5
Danish	33	5.4
English	8	1.7
Filipino	42	34.0
Finn	35	15.6
French	19	4.6
German	33	9.8
Greek	48	36.6
Hindu	82	66.2
Hungarian	52	27.3
Irish	10	4.7
Italian	43	19.3
Japanese	80	41.3
Mexican	49	45.9
Negro	26	30.3
Polish	35	24.4
Portuguese	52	22.3
Rumanian	51	26.6
Russian	45	22.9
Swedish	22	5.5
Turk	80	65.2

schools. Although the pattern is essentially the same, we can
rank the schools in terms of the general level of tolerance.
(This ranking must be tentative, since the anonymity of response was not controlled). Bennington and the two City College
samples were very tolerant for all of the groups on the list,
although the pattern of preference among these groups was essentially the same as the pattern at Howard and at "B," even
though the latter two were much more intolerant.

The level of the tolerance expressed by individuals is our
next concern. In their study of students' attitudes, Murphy and
Likert referred to a generalized tolerance factor, the score
for which was derived from a test very similar to the one used
here (12). They found that there was a high correlation between
the attitudes toward one-half the groups in the list, chosen at
random, and the attitudes towards the other half. In our test,
the order of presentation of the ethnic groups is alphabetical,
with the exception of French Canadians, who are juxtaposed to
Canadians instead of being listed with the F's. Separating the
thirty-two existing groups as they stand (omitting the non-
existent Danireans, Pireneans and Wallonians) taking them alternately we have 16 odd and 16 even groups. The attitude score,
as described in our discussion of the computation of the median
tolerance toward each group, was computed directly to get a
single general index of tolerance for the sixteen groups. This
was done separately for the odd and for the even groups. Then
correlation coefficients were computed between the two scores
for each individual -- the score for the odd and for the even
groups. This coefficient at "B," based on 66 cases, was .96. At
C.C.N.Y.--Business, for 126 students the coefficient was .95.
These indices are slightly higher than those reported by Murphy
and Likert, but the list used in this study is somewhat longer.
Apparently there is evidence to suggest that degree of tolerance expressed by individuals is a generalized function of the
individual and is not completely determined by the specific
group toward which the attitude is directed. There may be, of
course, much in the response of an individual which is determined by the specific group responded to, but the evidence for
the existence of the generalized tolerance suggests that it
might prove fruitful to explore it further.

Into the list of thirty-two existing groups, the three unfamiliar groups -- Danireans, Pireneans and Wallonians -- were
inserted in order to test the hypothesis concerning generalized
tolerance in a more concrete fashion. These groups sound plau-
sible, but as far as we know they do not correspond to any existing ethnic* designation. From the point of view of the experience of students, they must represent groups completely
unknown in reality. Even if some students may have chosen to
consider the Pireneans to be people who live in the Pyrenees;
the Wallonians, Walloons; and the Danireans something else; the
fact that they tended to do this is in itself significant. In
reality there are no such groups, and for the attributes an individual may assign to them, we must look to the individual for
the explanation, not to the group. Attitudes towards these
three groups should thus be test-tube samples of abstract tolerance-intolerance.

Within each of the samples, as we have already pointed out,
there are individuals who have different attitudes toward the
nationalities listed in the test. When we add up the tolerance
expressed for each of the thirty-two existing nations and races
by each individual in any one school sample, we find considerable variation in the total scores thus recorded. This variation represents the individual differences in tolerance expressed for a list of nations and races. Our hypothesis is that
such tolerance represents to a significant extent a function of
the persons responding, rather than of the groups responded to.
To test this hypothesis, we may correlate the average tolerance
for the thirty-two existing groups with the average tolerance
for the three "Nonesuch" groups (Danirean, Pirenean, Wallonian).
This correlation, computed separately in each school, should
give a critical test of our hypothesis. Our sample for these
correlations is unfortunately not quite as complete as might be
desired because some students refrained from responding to the
Nonesuch. The influence this might have had on the resulting
correlations will be discussed later. For the present let us

---

*In this report, the word "ethnic" will be used as a blanket
term to designate classification schemes based on race, religion, linguistics, or nationality.

consider the coefficients computed. Pearson product-moment coefficients of correlation were computed for five schools and
are presented in Table VII (see, also, Figures 2A, B, C). These
correlations range from .78 to .85 and confirm our hypothesis.

TABLE VII

Correlation between Mean Social Distance Scores Showing
Tolerance for Thirty-Two Existing Nations and Races
and for the Three Nonesuch Groups

School	r	PEr	n
Howard	.85	.02	(68)
"B"	.78	.03	(59)
"A"	.81	.03	(50)
Columbia	.81	.02	(101)
Bennington	.80	.05	(24)

This "test-tube" analysis of the generalized nature of tolerance would be inadequate without the consideration of the selec-
tive factors in a comparison of the individuals who responded to
the Nonesuch with those who omitted them. A study was made of
four different samples, comparing the total tolerance score towards the thirty-two existing groups of those who responded to,
and those who omitted response to the specific item of the Nonesuch selected. The samples and items chosen were arbitrarily selected to give an estimate of variability from school to school
and for the different items. Chi-square tests comparing the entire
distributions gave no evidence that would substantiate the hypothesis that those who omitted their response differed significantly in the degree of their general tolerance from those who
responded. A summary of these four comparisons is presented in
Table VIII.

This demonstration of the generalized nature of tolerance-
intolerance with respect to nations and races may be criticized
with the suggestions that the students are answering at random,
or that the students are trying to give the teacher what they
think the teacher wants. In answer to such criticism, it might

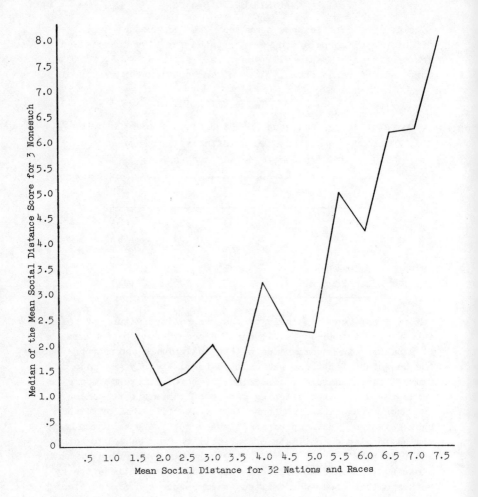

FIGURE 2A

School: "A"

Regression of attitude toward Nonesuch on attitude toward 32 existing groups. Median attitude toward Nonesuch of people holding different mean attitudes toward the existing groups. n = 50.

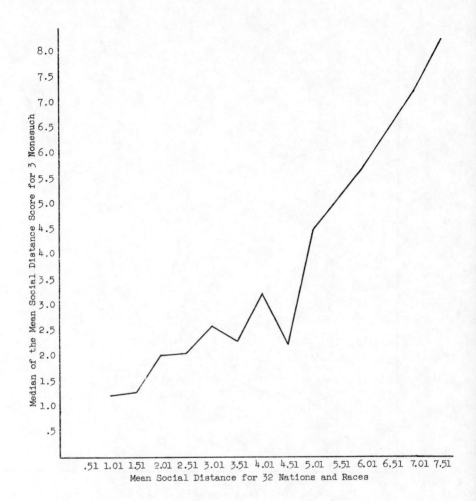

FIGURE 2B

School: HOWARD

Regression of attitude toward Nonesuch on attitude toward 32 existing groups.
Median attitude toward Nonesuch of people holding different mean attitudes toward
the existing groups. n = 68.

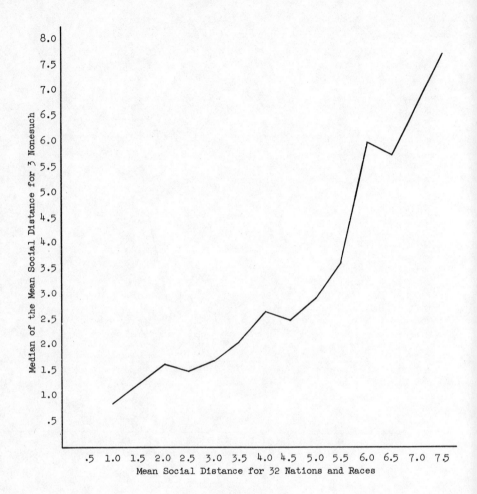

FIGURE 2C

School: COLUMBIA

Regression of attitude toward Nonesuch on attitude toward 32 existing groups.
Median attitude toward Nonesuch of people holding different mean attitudes toward
the existing groups. n = 101.

be pointed out that the differentiation among the groups made
by the students indicates that they were not answering completely at random. Further, the consistency of the hierarchy of
preferences shows that the pattern of answering was consonant
with what might be expected from college students in the United
States. On the whole, there is no reason to infer lack of faith
on the part of the students. Some of the students added margin
notes commenting on their responses. These comments showed very
clearly the relation between difference in response and differences among the respondent. We find one student writing to explain his attitude toward Danireans "I don't know anything
about them; therefore I would exclude them from my country."
And another student writing, "I don't know anything about them;
therefore I have no prejudices against them." (Both of these
students were at Columbia College.)

TABLE VIII

*Summary of Chi-Square Test of Hypothesis that Those Who Omitted
Response to Nonesuch Differed in Their Total Tolerance
Toward Existing Groups from Those Who Responded*

School Sample	No. responding	No. omitting	Item of Nonesuch	n	χ^2	P
Howard	60	14	Wallonian	3	8.2	.02 > .05
Columbia	86	48	Wallonian	3	4.8	.10 > .20
C.C.N.Y.- Arts	20	10	Pirenean	3	.34	.95 > .98
Bennington	19	12	Danirean	4	1.002	.80 > .90

Let us examine some further evidence supporting the validity
of the hypothesis that tolerance is highly generalized. At Howard University, a Negro institution where we might expect to
find very few, if any, Jewish students, the mean social distance
score for thirty-two nations and races for each of sixty-five
students was correlated against the sum of the social distance
scores for the three Jewish groups -- Russian Jews, German Jews,

and American Jews. The coefficient was computed by a product-
moment formula, and it was found that r = .72 (see Figure 3A).
At Howard, with sixty-one cases, the mean social distance score
of the students toward the three Nonesuch groups correlated .73
with tolerance for the three Jewish groups (see Fig. 3B). At
"B," eliminating those students who were either Jews or did not
identify themselves with any religious group listed, we find
among thirty "Christian" students the correlation coefficient
between mean tolerance for the Nonesuch and tolerance for Jews
was r = .59. If the attitude toward Jews is so significantly
correlated with tolerance for Nonesuch groups, it seems a little difficult to try to account for an individual's attitude
toward Jews on the basis of the characteristics of the Jewish
group.

It is clearly recognized that for any correlation coefficient
a coefficient of alienation may be computed, and that there
does exist a difference in attitudes exhibited toward Jews and
Nonesuch groups. But there seems to be a large common element
determining the responses of the students to both. Further correlations were computed to explore the extent of the operation
of the generalized tolerance factor. Tolerances were inter-cor-
related for Negroes and Jews, Jews and Catholics, Catholics and
Negroes, and between Nonesuch groups and each of the following:
Jew, Catholic, Communist, Fascist, C.I.O. Organizer, and Labor
Union member. These correlations appear in Table IX as found in
the samples from Columbia and Bennington. In each correlation
care was taken to select individuals who reported no affiliation with any of the groups involved in the particular relationship study. In the correlation, for example, of tolerance for
Jews and Catholics, only the responses of Protestant students
were examined (see, also, Figure 4).

The significance of the evidence for generalization of the
attitude expressed towards various groups included in this sur-
vey may be seen more analytically in the following study of the
relationship between tolerance for Communists and tolerance for
Fascists. In the small group of political designations item 44
was "Communist" and item 45, "Fascist." The students at the
different schools indicated their reaction toward both items
along with the other forty-seven. Scatter-diagrams of the re-

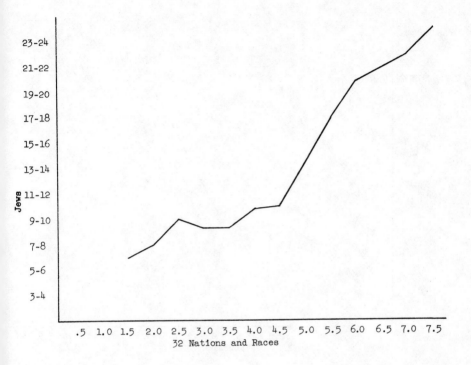

FIGURE 3A

School: HOWARD

Regression of tolerance for Jews on mean social distance score for 32 nations
and races. Median of the sums of social distance indications for the 3 Jewish
groups for different mean social distance scores for the 32 ethnic groups.

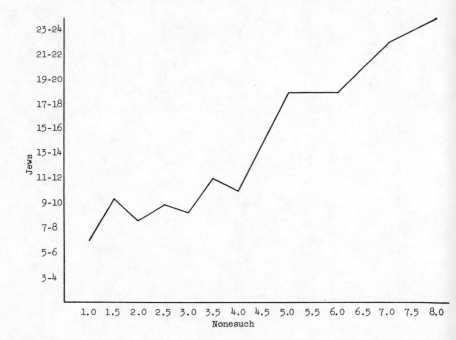

FIGURE 3B

School: HOWARD

Regression of tolerance for Jews on tolerance for Nonesuch. Median of the sums of social distance indications for the 3 Jewish groups for different mean social distance scores for the 3 Nonesuch.

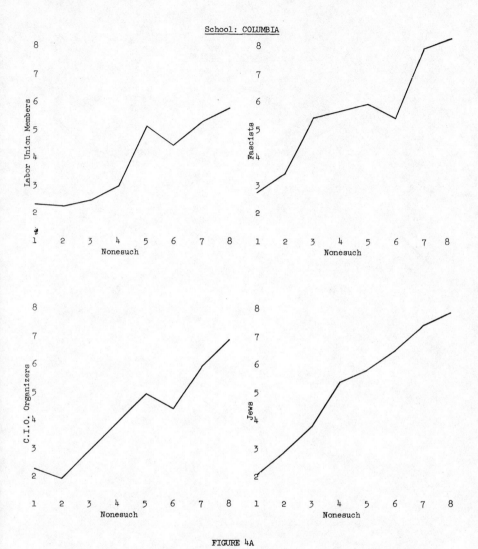

School: COLUMBIA

FIGURE 4A

Graphic demonstration of the generalized nature of tolerance. In each of the charts the curve represents the median of the tolerance for the group designated by the ordinate as a function of tolerance for the group indicated on the abscissa.

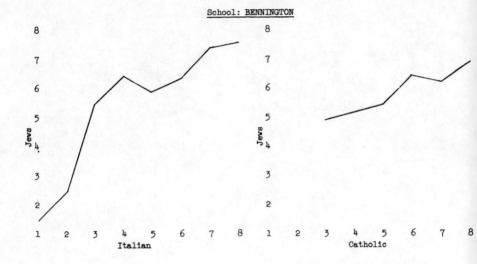

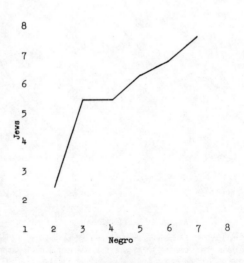

FIGURE 4B

Graphic demonstration of the generalized nature of tolerance. In each of the charts the curve represents the median of the tolerance for the group designated by the ordinate as a function of tolerance for the group indicated on the abscissa.

sponses by the students at five of the schools showed an interesting relationship between tolerance for these two groups.
These scatter-diagrams for Princeton, "A," Howard, Columbia,
and C.C.N.Y.--Business are reproduced in Figure 5. The linearity of the relationship between tolerance for these two groups
is quite striking. At Princeton, we find 67 out of 77 students
assigning a tolerance rank for one group within one point on
the scale of their tolerance for the other. At "A," 52 out of
59 give that close an approximation; at Howard, 52 out of 64;
Columbia, 80 of 119; and C.C.N.Y.--Business, 72 of 122.

TABLE IX

The Generalized Nature of Tolerance Correlations of Responses
to Selected Items in the Social Distance Test at
Columbia and Bennington

Correlation	Columbia		Bennington	
	r	n	r	n
Negro--Jew	.68	59	.68	27
Jew--Catholic	.52	29	.21	26
Catholic--Negro	.53	44	---	--
Jew--Italian	.42	51	.65	27
Nonesuch--Jew	.63	51	.55	22
Nonesuch--Catholic	.41	56	.35	22
Communist--Nonesuch	.68	96	.52	24
Fascist--Nonesuch	.59	94	.23	24
C.I.O. Organizer--Nonesuch	.60	96	.57	24
Labor Union Member--Nonesuch	.58	95	.43	24

If we divide our scatter-diagrams into quadrants drawing lines
of demarcation between steps 4 and 5, we have a convenient focus
for discussion. Through step 4, admission "to employment in my
occupation in my country" represents a degree of tolerance which
is somewhat artificial for college students. Steps 5, 6, 7, and
8, referring to classmates, neighbors, chums, and kin, are much
nearer and much more personal than occupational employment and

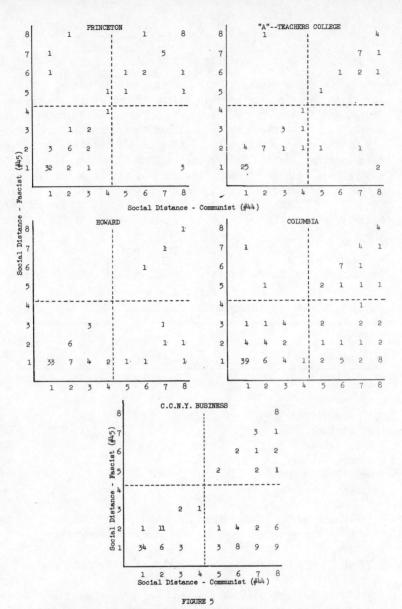

FIGURE 5

Chart showing scatter diagrams of correlation between tolerance for Communists and tolerance for Fascists at five different schools. Note, at Columbia and C.C.N.Y., the concentration in quadrant representing pro-Communist - anti-Fascist; at the same time the linearity of the tolerance function is emphasized by the majority of the students.

the greater degrees of social distance. The opposition between
the philosophies of the Fascists and Communists has led many to
believe that individuals are to be classified as either pro-
Fascists - anti-Communists, or pro-Communists - anti-Fascists.

If, in our scatter-diagrams, we consider the line between
steps 4 and 5 to be the dividing line between "pro" and "anti,"
admittedly a highly arbitrary procedure, we may get some indication of the extent to which individuals tend to be pro-one
anti-the other or pro-pro and anti-anti, which is the organization of attitude one would expect from the hypothesis of generalized tolerance-intolerance. At Princeton, we find 7 of the 77
are pro-one, anti-the other. At "A" this number is 5 out of 59;
at Howard, 12 out of 64; at Columbia, 31 out of 119; at C.C.N.Y.
--Business, 41 out of 122. In the progression of the charts, an
increasing concentration of expression of tolerance for Communists, intolerance for Fascists may be seen. In all schools
these individuals are decidedly in the minority.

In the first two charts this concentration is sufficiently
slight to suggest that it may readily be discounted as a distinct factor in the sample as a whole, though in actual social
influence, we cannot estimate the effects of any individuals on
the basis of this sort of examination. In the last two charts
it seems quite clear that the concentration of students in the
pro-Communist - anti-Fascist quadrant is sufficient to suggest
heterogeneity of the sample. This seems to show that on the
whole the generalized nature of tolerance is a principle which
would apply even to tolerance for Communists and Fascists
though under special circumstances attitudes can be so affected
as to induce variation, and introduce, from the statistical
point of view, heterogeneity into what might otherwise be considered a homogeneous college sample. That this heterogeneity
can exist demonstrates that under appropriate influences the
principle of generalized tolerance may be destroyed and individuals can respond with specialized differentiations.

This material cannot be interpreted as an index of the attitude towards Fascism and Communism, but only as indication of
attitude toward Fascists and Communists. There is undoubtedly
a relationship between attitude toward "ism" and "ist," but it
is the tolerance for the people rather than the ideas that con-

cern us in this study. We are not as much concerned about non-
Catholics' ideas of Catholicism or their susceptibility to Catholic theology as we are interested in the tolerance of people
for Catholics; not so much interested in the possibilities of
proselytizing among Whites to convert them to "Negroism," as we
are interested in the tolerance of Whites for Negroes.

The questionnaire used in this study makes no pretense of giving an accurate basis for prediction of all possible behavior
of the respondent in relationship to members of each of the
groups included in the test. The test represents a controlled
situation in which students had an opportunity to indicate
fairly clearly the degree of tolerance they would display. Thus
while any one student gives evidence concerning his tendency to
discriminate among peoples, we also have an opportunity to compare two students in terms of the level of tolerance they display in controlled conditions. If student A says "I would refuse
citizenship to Arabs" and student B says "I would admit Arabs to
my group as personal chums," we cannot really be sure that in a
test case A would really refuse an Arab citizenship, nor could
we be sure that B would really admit an Arab to his group as a
chum. We can be pretty sure, however, that under any comparable
circumstances B on the whole would probably be more tolerant of
Arabs than A. Our confidence that this is so is a function of
our acceptance of the response on the questionnaire, not as a
statement of attitude, but as a sample of behavior of the two
students under controlled conditions.

There seems to be a general American tradition of preference
for members of certain ethnic groups, which tradition is accepted by college students. Just where in the general scale of
tolerance this order is pegged seems to be a function of the
particular group studied. On the basis of our analysis of college students' behavior under the controlled conditions of the
questionnaire, it seems that response to any particular ethnic
group is to some extent a function of the generalized degree of
tolerance-intolerance which is characteristic of the particular
respondent. The precise extent varies with the particular group,
but in no case does this factor seem to be insignificant. Within
any one sample there is considerably variation in the tolerance
of individuals, and this tolerance seems to be a generalized
function of the individual.

CHAPTER III

TOLERANCE AND OTHER FRAMES OF REFERENCE

MANY EXPERIMENTS antedating the present study suggest that race attitudes may be conceived as frameworks within which people respond. Orienting either from an elaboration of Stuart Rice's "stereotypes" (14) or Sherif's "frame of reference" (15) or from any other systematic position, it would be important to study the general constellation in the light of which tolerance as an aspect of personality may be viewed.

An approach to the frameworks within which individuals respond was undertaken in almost completely perceptual terms. How is the world organized for the respondents? What things go together, what things are separate? We cannot be sure that a priori, logical analyses give accurate psychological descriptions. If we study the ways in which individuals organize social phenomena, get clues to their general approach to the world, find out what things they classify together and what things they consider different, we might have a more adequate understanding of the bases for their responses. If a test could be devised to get an objective demonstration of the way in which the world is organized for different individuals, we might then try to relate the types of organization to manifestations of tolerance. This chapter presents the results of some studies designed in accordance with this perspective.

After a few experimental records had been informally studied, a new test was prepared involving eighty-one pairs of words as shown in Figures 6A and 6B. Individuals were asked to indicate whether they felt that the two words of each pair tended to be "similar" or "dissimilar." All pairs could be labeled either way with justification. The pairs included were of the order of (1) paint--oil, (9) 1 minute--75 seconds, (18) Catholic--Protestant, (45) employer--employee. These word pairs were selected in order to gain insight into the frameworks of what might be called

ethnic elements: word pairs including different ethnic terms,
e.g. Item 29, German--Italian

flexibility: word pairs including words representing different ways of doing the same thing, generally terms
taken to provide equivalents from different cul-
tures, e.g. Item 56, dress--sarong; Item 64, toma-
hawk--hatchet.

sex: words representing one masculine and one feminine term
for equivalent elements, e.g. Item 50, actor--ac-
tress; Item 60, widow--widower.

economic: words included to give an approach to understanding
of various elements within our socio-economic system, e.g. Item 6, bourgeois--proletariat; Item 61,
borrower--lender.

school: words selected to give understanding of the approach
to the school situation, e.g. Item 8, classmate--
competitor; Item 21, education--struggle.

parental attitude: words selected to give approach to understanding of the conceptions of parents, e.g. Item
42, father--policeman; Item 77, mother--Victorian.

Other word pairs were inserted to test various other incidental
hypotheses. Two forms of the test were prepared. On Form One,
just described, students had the choice of labeling a word pair
"similar" or "dissimilar" (Fig. 6A). The second form called for
rating of the word pairs on a five-point scale which offered
two degrees of similarity, two degrees of dissimilarity, and
one midpoint representing the attitude that the respondent
could not judge the words as similar or dissimilar (Fig. 6B).
These two forms are presented in full in Figures 6A and 6B respectively.

Form One was the first page of the three-page test booklet
distributed for the collection of data in all schools except
the C.C.N.Y. samples. Of the standard three-page leaflet, page
2 was the social distance test illustrated in Figure 1. Page 3
was the equivalent of page 2 except that it offered students
the opportunity of encircling I, F or M (standing for self,
father, and mother) instead of numbers (Fig. 1A). C.C.N.Y.--
Business sample did not take the similarity-dissimilarity test.
The C.C.N.Y.--Arts sample took both forms; half of the group
(one section of the two elementary classes taught by the co-

FIGURE 6A

Name:_____ Sex:_____ School Year:_____ Date:_____

DIRECTIONS. Below are a number of pairs of words. Consider each pair carefully and decide whether in general the elements are similar or dissimilar. If on the whole you would tend to call the two more alike than different, put an S (for same or similar) on the line before the pair. If you would tend to think of them as more different than similar, put a D (for different or dissimilar) on the line before the pair. Work as rapidly as possible and GIVE YOUR FIRST IMPRESSIONS.

1___Paint--Oil	28___Rooster--Hen	55___Fool--Carefree
2___Aspirin--Advertising	29___German--Italian	56___Dress--Sarong
3___Circle--Triangle	30___Mary--Moses	57___Judge--Mother
4___Boy--Girl	31___Mexico--United States	58___Factory--Shop
5___Hello--Hullo	32___Fork--Chop Sticks	59___French--German
6___Bourgeois--Proletariat	33___Rival--Colleague	60___Widow--Widower
7___One O'clock--Five Past One	34___Poor Man--Rich Man	61___Borrower--Lender
8___Classmate--Competitor	35___Fly--Butterfly	62___China--Spain
9___1 Minute--75 Seconds	36___Seamstress--Tailor	63___Apples--Nuts
10___Consumer--Manufacturer	37___Non-aryan--Aryan	64___Tomahawk--Hatchet
11___Catholic--English	38___Aunt--Uncle	65___Turban--Hat
12___Witch Doctor--Physician	39___Alligator--Crocodile	66___Canada--Portugal
13___Mother--Father	40___Italian--Russian	67___Husband--Wife
14___Pickled Herring--Fish Cakes	41___Freedom--Job	68___River--Ocean
15___5 Minutes--10 Minutes	42___Father--Policeman	69___2:40 P.M.--2:50 P.M.
16___Battleground--College	43___Square--Circle	70___Old Man--Father
17___Cow--Bull	44___Italian--Jew	71___Good By--Au Revoir
18___Catholic--Protestant	45___Employer--Employee	72___Negro--Irish
19___Factory Worker--Farmer	46___Friend--Classmate	73___Maker--Seller
20___Competition--Cooperation	47___Chop Suey--Beef Stew	74___Student--Worker
21___Education--Struggle	48___Serious--Trustworthy	75___Oranges--Tangerines
22___John--Joan	49___Christian--Jew	76___White--Negro
23___Japanese--Chinese	50___Actor--Actress	77___Mother--Victorian
24___Job--Responsibility	51___Tenant--Landlord	78___Club--Union
25___Pork Chops--Roast Beef	52___Nephew--Niece	79___Wealth--Success
26___Barber--Manicurist	53___Jew--American	80___Man--Woman
27___Internationalist--Patriot	54___Dog--Cat	81___Smile--Grin

Please make sure you have entered a judgment for each pair. If you care to add any comments, use the space below and the back of this sheet, if necessary.

FIGURE 6B

Name:_____ Class:_____ Date:_____

DIRECTIONS. Below are a number of pairs of words. Consider each pair carefully and judge the degree of general similarity or dissimilarity of the elements. Enter your estimates on the line before each pair in accordance with this scheme:

       0 means you feel that they are very similar
       1 means you feel they tend toward similarity

       3 means you feel thay tend toward dissimilarity
       4 means you feel they are very dissimilar

       2 means you feel you cannot judge them as similar or dissimilar

1___Paint--Oil	28___Rooster--Hen	55___Fool--Carefree
2___Aspirin--Advertising	29___German--Italian	56___Dress--Sarong
3___Circle--Triangle	30___Mary--Moses	57___Judge--Mother
4___Boy--Girl	31___Mexico--United States	58___Factory--Shop
5___Hello--Hullo	32___Fork--Chop Sticks	59___French--German
6___Bourgeois--Proletariat	33___Rival--Colleague	60___Widow--Widower
7___One O'clock--Five Past One	34___Poor Man--Rich Man	61___Borrower--Lender
8___Classmate--Competitor	35___Fly--Butterfly	62___China--Spain
9___1 Minute--75 Seconds	36___Seamstress--Tailor	63___Apples--Nuts
10___Consumer--Manufacturer	37___Non-aryan--Aryan	64___Tomahawk--Hatchet
11___Catholic--English	38___Aunt--Uncle	65___Turban--Hat
12___Witch Doctor--Physician	39___Alligator--Crocodile	66___Canada--Portugal
13___Mother--Father	40___Italian--Russian	67___Husband--Wife
14___Pickled Herring--Fish Cakes	41___Freedom--Job	68___River--Ocean
15___5 Minutes--10 Minutes	42___Father--Policeman	69___2:40 P.M.--2:50 P.M.
16___Battleground--College	43___Square--Circle	70___Old Man--Father
17___Cow--Bull	44___Italian--Jew	71___Good Bye--Au Revoir
18___Catholic--Protestant	45___Employer--Employee	72___Negro--Irish
19___Factory Worker--Farmer	46___Friend--Classmate	73___Maker--Seller
20___Competition--Cooperation	47___Chop Suey--Beef Stew	74___Student--Worker
21___Education--Struggle	48___Serious--Trustworthy	75___Oranges--Tangerines
22___John--Joan	49___Christian--Jew	76___White--Negro
23___Japanese--Chinese	50___Actor--Actress	77___Mother--Victorian
24___Job--Responsibility	51___Tenant--Landlord	78___Club--Union
25___Pork Chops--Roast Beef	52___Nephew--Niece	79___Wealth--Success
26___Barber--Manicurist	53___Jew--American	80___Man--Woman
27___Internationalist--Patriot	54___Dog--Cat	81___Smile--Grin

Please make sure you have entered a judgment for each pair. If you care to add any comments, use the space below and the back of the sheet.

operating instructor) took the test with Form One first; the
other half took it with Form Two first. The tests were repeated
after an interval of a month, with appropriate changes in forms,
so that each student took a different form of the similarity-
dissimilarity test at the second testing.

On the basis of the re-test materials at C.C.N.Y.--Arts, reliability coefficients for each item were computed. The dichoto-
mous nature of the responses to Form One were made equivalent to
the five-point scale of Form Two by omitting from consideration
responses on the latter which indicated that the respondent
felt the pair could not be judged, and disregarding the degrees
represented in the responses similar or dissimilar. Tetrachoric
correlating coefficients were computed from the Chesire, Saffir,
Thurstone computing diagrams (3) and are presented in Table X.
Correlations were not computed for items 16, 17, 18, 19, 20, 21,
22, 24, 27, 33, 34, 39, 45, 51. The distribution of responses
in these cases was such that one of the quadrants had so few
cases that any estimate would be too unreliable to warrant inclusion in the table. Limits for inclusion were determined by
the computing diagrams; those distributions which were so extreme as to have no diagram appropriate, were omitted from consideration here. The variability of the reliability coefficients indicated that responses to all items cannot be accepted
with equal confidence.

Since our interest is in those frameworks which might be related to tolerance, two of the most tolerant schools and two of
the most intolerant schools were chosen for further study. The
response of the students at Howard and "B" (the intolerant
schools), and C.C.N.Y.--Arts and Bennington (the tolerant
schools) to each item were studied. Table XI gives a recapitu-
lation of the responses of the students at each of these four
schools to each item expressed as the percentage of each sample
responding "similar" to the particular word pair.

Forty-two items were selected for further study based upon
consideration of the reliability coefficients, the comparison
of the distribution of students at the relatively tolerant and
intolerant schools and the emergent hypotheses. Each of these
items was separately correlated in each of the four schools
against the general mean social distance scores discussed pre-

TABLE X

Reliability Coefficients for Each Item of the Similar-Dissimilar Test Computed as Tetrachoric Correlation Coefficients Based on a One Month Re-Test

Item	Coefficient	Item	Coefficient
1	.20	41	.30
2	.30	42	.95
3	.50	43	.90
4	.50	44	.50
5	.90	45	--
6	.80	46	.30
7	.40	47	.30
8	.30	48	.50
9	.30	49	.40
10	.10	50	.30
11	.40	51	--
12	.80	52	.10
13	.30	53	.40
14	.50	54	.20
15	.20	55	.70
16	--*	56	.00
17	--	57	.50
18	--	58	.50
19	--	59	.60
20	--	60	.30
21	--	61	.90
22	--	62	.70
23	.40	63	.70
24	--	64	.80
25	.40	65	.50
26	.90	66	.50
27	--	67	.20
28	.30	68	.50
29	.90	69	.10
30	.75	70	.60
31	.40	71	.60
32	.90	72	.60
33	--	73	.30
34	--	74	.40
35	.30	75	.60
36	.40	76	.80
37	.60	77	.80
38	.00	78	.10
39	--	79	.40
40	70	80	.00
		81	.60

*Indicates distributions did not admit estimation of correlation by the method used.

TABLE XI

*Percentage of Sample Responding "Similar" to Each Item of the
Similar-Dissimilar Test in Four Schools*

Item	Howard	"B"	C.C.N.Y. Arts	Bennington
1. Paint--Oil	80	76	86	81
2. Aspirin--Advertising	13	12	44	13
3. Circle--Triangle	42	18	43	35
4. Boy--Girl	49	32	40	33
5. Hello--Hullo	80	91	96	84
6. Bourgeois--Proletariat	35	45	29	65
7. One o'clock--Five Past One	52	61	57	52
8. Classmate--Competitor	44	38	46	23
9. 1 Minute--75 Seconds	47	32	39	45
10. Consumer--Manufacturer	42	25	20	29
11. Catholic--English	20	15	11	23
12. Witch Doctor--Physician	46	35	16	23
13. Mother--Father	66	49	77	45
14. Pickled Herring--Fish Cakes	43	45	36	48
15. 5 Minutes--10 Minutes	49	48	39	39
16. Battleground--College	12	15	4	0
17. Cow--Bull	74	46	60	52
18. Catholic--Protestant	49	49	50	39
19. Factory Worker--Farmer	43	27	46	35
20. Competition--Cooperation	14	9	6	3
21. Education--Struggle	63	48	62	23
22. John--Jean	48	47	64	61
23. Japanese--Chinese	64	77	67	61
24. Job--Responsibility	89	84	93	87
25. Pork Chops--Roast Beef	49	53	56	45
26. Barber--Manicurist	55	59	64	45
27. Internationalist--Patriot	32	27	7	23
28. Rooster--Hen	76	45	52	48
29. German--Italian	42	38	36	42
30. Mary--Moses	40	33	14	26
31. Mexico--United States	41	36	30	23
32. Fork--Chop Sticks	78	58	70	45
33. Rival--Colleague	27	14	3	10
34. Poor Man--Rich Man	37	21	7	23
35. Fly--Butterfly	63	52	47	42
36. Seamstress--Tailor	96	89	94	90
37. Non-aryan--Aryan	20	23	32	29
38. Aunt--Uncle	71	55	77	58
39. Alligator--Crocodile	93	88	90	90
40. Italian--Russian	33	21	22	16

TABLE XI (Continued)

*Percentage of Sample Responding "Similar" to Each Item of the
Similar-Dissimilar Test in Four Schools*

Item	Howard	"B"	C.C.N.Y. Arts	Bennington
41. Freedom--Job	24	18	18	29
42. Father--Policeman	27	14	17	3
43. Square--Circle	42	12	31	29
44. Italian--Jew	34	17	32	23
45. Employer--Employee	38	33	10	29
46. Friend--Classmate	89	82	90	90
47. Chop Suey--Beef Stew	50	48	43	42
48. Serious--Trustworthy	47	50	59	71
49. Christian--Jew	33	36	38	29
50. Actor--Actress	85	73	86	84
51. Tenant--Landlord	38	30	17	23
52. Nephew--Niece	76	67	80	61
53. Jew--American	41	35	73	35
54. Dog--Cat	53	39	36	45
55. Fool--Carefree	63	52	59	32
56. Dress--Sarong	51	38	62	55
57. Judge--Mother	25	18	27	6
58. Factory--Shop	78	91	90	35
59. French--German	36	35	37	52
60. Widow--Widower	79	56	69	81
61. Borrower--Lender	36	23	17	39
62. China--Spain	42	24	55	23
63. Apples--Nuts	21	20	35	45
64. Tomahawk--Hatchet	89	92	86	97
65. Turban--Hat	97	86	93	90
66. Canada--Portugal	33	12	26	6
67. Husband--Wife	63	47	80	61
68. River--Ocean	73	33	59	35
69. 2:40 P.M.--2:50 P.M.	50	52	50	55
70. Old Man--Father	47	41	44	16
71. Good Bye--Au Revoir	92	95	94	94
72. Negro--Irish	28	9	14	10
73. Maker--Seller	53	38	52	32
74. Student--Worker	61	56	64	61
75. Oranges--Tangerines	67	89	86	84
76. White--Negro	37	14	27	29
77. Mother--Victorian	23	24	17	19
78. Wealth--Success	77	62	73	42
79. Club--Union	84	64	69	48
80. Man--Woman	50	32	52	48
81. Smile--Grin	93	89	87	77

TABLE XII

Bi-Serial Correlation Coefficients between Tendency to Say Similar
to Each of Forty-Two Items on the Similar-Dissimilarity Test
and the Tendency to Be Tolerant toward Nations and Races

Positive correlations indicate tendency to say similar is
associated with tendency to be more tolerant.

Item	Bennington	"B"	Howard	C.C.N.Y.--Arts
6	-.11	.07	.51	.30
9	-.22	-.14	-.27	.10
12	-.51	-.14	.17	.07
13	-.22	-.09	.41	.00
15	-.28	-.42	.10	-.10
16	.00	-.26	-.05	-.49
18	-.20	-.05	.47	.19
20	-.79	.29	.39	-.08
21	.21	-.06	.13	.07
22	.00	-.07	.18	-.09
25	-.31	.72	.10	-.36
27	-.51	-.16	.28	-.05
29	.00	-.22	.41	.25
30	.42	-.09	.32	.37
31	-.10	-.03	.33	.04
33	-.42	.26	-.07	.57
34	-.15	.11	.08	.26
35	-.29	-.34	.13	-.35
37	-.11	.08	-.16	.33
40	.13	-.11	.35	.52
42	.12	-.07	-.19	.13
44	.51	-.32	.35	.48
45	.11	-.15	.23	-.14
46	.66	.09	.38	-.77
47	.21	.07	.29	-.38
48	.12	.20	-.18	-.58
49	.17	.09	.28	.30
51	-.05	.01	.31	.13
53	.06	.05	.24	.09
56	.65	.03	.00	.00
57	-.30	-.17	-.12	-.40
58	.06	-.33	.44	-.51
59	--	-.05	.30	.20
63	.23	.09	.56	.05
67	.00	.34	.13	.00
70	-.09	-.15	-.27	-.32
75	.00	-.44	.00	-.41
77	.23	-.32	-.11	.16
78	.07	-.03	.28	-.19
79	-.21	-.13	.20	-.19
80	-.07	.07	.10	-.13
81	.00	.25	-.56	.00

49

viously as an index of general tolerance. The bi-serial correlation coefficients are presented in Table XII. This table was
studied for consistency of the sign of correlation at the different schools and those items where the correlations were all
like-signed, or were like-signed with a zero coefficient, were
selected. When studied in this fashion, the forty-two items
showed results of sufficient variability to eliminate all but
nine from further discussion here. These items are reviewed in
Table XIII.

TABLE XIII

*Items Selected from Table XII in Which Coefficients
Are Like–Signed*

Item	Bennington	"B"	Howard	CCNY-Arts
16. Battleground--College	.30	-.26	.05	-.49
49. Christian--Jew	.17	.09	.28	.30
53. Jew--American	.06	.05	.24	.09
56. Dress--Sarong	.65	.03	.00	.00
57. Judge--Mother	-.30	-.17	-.12	-.40
63. Apples--Nuts	.23	.09	.56	.05
67. Husband--Wife	.00	.34	.13	.00
70. Old Man--Father	-.09	-.15	-.27	-.32
75. Oranges--Tangerines	.00	-.44	.00	-.41

In spite of the unsatisfactory reliability coefficients reported for some of the items in Table X, it seems worth considering the implications of these correlations to illustrate
the possible fruitfulness of this experimental approach to the
structuring of attitudes. The discussion proceeds on the assumption that some tentative hypotheses may prove of significance if only as stimulation to criticism and further research.

A first hypothesis is: People who tend to emphasize the essential similarity of people of different religions (or other
ethnic groupings) are more tolerant than those who respond with
emphasis on the differences.

If we consider the tendency to answer "Similar" to items 57 and 70 evidence of relatively unsatisfactory adjustment to parents, we may postulate that: With lack of satisfactory parent-child relationship at the college level, there tends to be relatively more intolerance.

Items 56, 63 and 75 might be expected to offer a clue to the significance of the "flexibility" factor. That negative correlations emerge from 75 and positive from 56 and 63, lends added emphasis to the caution and tentativeness with which these hypotheses should be taken. For the sake of providing a point of departure, however tentative, let us suggest that: If one can accept different ways of doing things as equivalents, one is inclined to be more tolerant of peoples of different nations and races.

Though open to many interpretations, we shall choose to emphasize the sex feature of the differentiation in item 67. The fact that we are relying on only two positive correlations coupled with two zero coefficients makes us very hesitant, but in the light of the nature of the purpose of this series of hypotheses, we shall suggest for consideration the proposition that: People for whom sex is not particularly important tend to be relatively tolerant.

The final offering stems from item 16 and may be formulated: Among those students whose backgrounds permit them to conceive college as a relatively non-aggressive, non-competitive place, there is greater tolerance for people of various nations and races.

The behavior of human beings is sufficiently variable to provide the research workers with many problems. In a "shot gun" type study where many items are included for analysis, on a purely random basis responses will tend to accumulate on particular items to serve as "statistically significant" elements in the analysis of some worker. We should not pay much attention to unexpected findings which develop from an analysis which starts by selecting for further assay those elements which give most promise of demonstrating a difference. It seems appropriate to concentrate only on those factors which are not functions of chance phenomena and are involved in the a priori hypotheses. The similar-dissimilar test was originally constructed so that

it included possible test of several hypotheses. Unfortunately,
there was not sufficient time adequately to standardize the
items and refine the words used and equate the pairs to make
the present results other than suggestive. The technique seems
fruitful and the findings discussed above are not without implications, and not necessarily to be completely discarded. Few
of them seem surprising, which might be taken as evidence that
they represent confirmation of hypotheses that are generally
acceptable. It is hoped that their presentation here in juxta-
position with the hypotheses will lead to clarification of further thinking for more fruitful approaches to study.

In this discussion there is no wish to minimize the importance of the doubts raised by the statistical analyses concerning the possibilities for generalizing from the evidence at
hand. Not only must we emphasize the limitations imposed on our
discussion by the statistical findings, but there are the more
direct limitations based upon the sampling and the nature of
the test to be considered. The factors of perseverative tendencies, the space order of the arrangements, all should be carefully analyzed. Unfortunately, the present study could not undertake the necessary program. We may consider the analysis to
have yielded some points which merit consideration and the technique seems, to the present writer, one which merits further
exploration.

CHAPTER IV

TOLERANCE AND PERSONALITY TRAITS

The Preliminary Study of Personality Sketches

ANALYSIS OF ETHNIC TOLERANCE in relation to other "frameworks" of an individual is of interest but is by no means the only approach to the understanding of attitudes. If attitude toward one particular group is in part a function of a broader, deeper tolerance, presumably other specific attitudes might be representations of broader, deeper functions. Clinical study of individuals from a psychological point of view seems to offer some fairly fundamental approach in the perspective of which it might be desirable to study tolerance. At C.C.N.Y.--Arts, students in two sections of a general psychology class from whom the attitude test material had been collected were asked, some time later, in a manner which indicated absolutely no relation to the race attitude material, to prepare a description of their "personality" as an assignment. The students were provided with an outline prepared for this study:

Outline for Study of Individual as a Social Unit

Each person has an individuality which is unique, which represents an organization of characteristics which is probably precisely duplicated in no other person in the world. There are, of course, many elements in personality which are common to a wide number of people, but we are here interested in the patterning of elements which represents the individuality of the individual.

Please consider each section below carefully. Read the questions, then please discuss yourself in the light of those questions. Don't try merely to answer each specific query, elaborate upon the theme involved. Cover the different points raised, but don't limit yourself, don't restrict your discussion to the questions as stated. Present all relevant material in detail. In case of doubt about material to include, remember that it is better to put in more than less.

1. What are your skills? What are you good at and what are you poor at? Consider school, outside of school, home, leisure

time activities, hobbies, vocationally useful aptitudes. What
do you enjoy doing? What do you find unpleasant? Describe fully,
giving details contributing to enjoyment, to lack of enjoyment.
What would you like to be able to do better to secure more enjoyment.

2. What is your general approach to your associates? How
spontaneous are you in your relations with them? To what extent
do you hold back? Consider boys and girls separately. Under
what circumstances are you most free? With what sort of people?
Least free? Who are your intimates? What factors entered into
your selection of each of them? How did you become acquainted,
how did the friendship develop? What do you like about each?
What do you dislike about them? List six people you can't stand
having anything to do with. Describe each of them. What is
there about each that you dislike? List six people whom you
know who seem to be all right but with whom you wouldn't care
to become intimate. Describe each. What is it you like about
each? Why do you feel you would not like to know them better?
Discuss each one separately, at length, and probe into the
"Why's" of your statements.

3. What is your general reaction to those slightly younger
than yourself? Considerably older? Do you consider yourself an
adult or an adolescent? How does this self-evaluation affect
your relations to others? Are you accepted at the level you
consider yourself? Who does, who doesn't? What circumstances
make you feel young? When do you feel old?

4. Where do you feel "at home"? With whom? What groups do you
feel a member of? Identified with? Where, with whom do you feel
you do not belong? What difficulties are introduced by these
feelings of belongingness and not belonging? Discuss in detail,
citing examples and describing instances.

5. When, under what circumstances are you most confident of
yourself? Least confident? What specific fears bother you? How
much do they disturb you (be specific)? In what ways do they
interfere?

6. Describe situations in which you have inner conflicts, are
drawn in two or more opposing directions. What are the bases of
these conflicts? Which aspects generally win? Under what circumstances may the other aspects dominate?

7. When are you happiest? If you had a magic wishing wand and
could wish for absolutely anything, what might you ask for?
Discuss at length. What will Heaven be like? What will you be
like in Heaven? Who else will be there? Who won't be there?
(If you do not believe in life after death, say so and develop
this theme through fantasy.) What sort of thing makes you unhappy?

8. When do you feel tense, anxious, upset? Discuss how these feelings develop, describing the circumstances in typical cases, and how they recede. What factors create tension? Describe at least three situations, the most recent you can recall, in which you felt dis⁺inctly uncomfortable. Discuss the phases which contributed to your discomfort.

9. (Summary) For you, what seems to be the fundamental organizations of life, into what major categories is living organized from your point of view? From your point of view, how are activities classified? How do you classify things? How do you classify people? Discuss in detail, citing examples.

It will be noticed that the outline makes no particular ethnic references, although it permits such reference if the student is inclined to include it. Thirty-four students turned in case discriptions in accordance with this outline. With the leeway permitted in the directions, many students departed radically in their personality sketches from the precise questions presented. The responses were then transcribed on the typewriter so that they provided a uniform appearance, all errors of spelling and grammar were retained. The names of the authors were deleted and code numbers assigned. On the basis of the mean social distance score for thirty-two nations and races previously recorded, the thirty-four individuals were assigned rank positions for tolerance. They were then sorted into two groups taken alternately from the ranking. These two groups were thus of comparable composition, from the point of view of general tolerance for nations and races, and not specially selected with respect to personality. The two groups, of seventeen studies each, were ready for study. Precautions were taken to maintain the anonymity of the authors of the sketches and to prevent any clues to the other material available on the students from being available in the typewritten copies of the personality sketches.

Each of two advanced students of psychology was asked to arrange one of the series of seventeen sketches in a rank order of general racial tolerance. Both were given insight into the conception of generalized tolerance as it has been developed in this paper, although the relationship between tolerance and other attitudes as discussed in the similarity-dissimilarity tests was not available. Each rater had complete freedom of

choice concerning the methods to be used and the basis for prediction of tolerance. To secure careful consideration of the
material not only was interest induced in the raters, but minor
remuneration was provided. When the rankings were completed,
rank difference correlation coefficients were computed to present a quantitative estimate of the success of each rater.
These coefficients were, for rater one, -.22, and for rater two,
+.74. Apparently one rater had considerable success and the
other none.

Without being told about their relative success, both raters
were asked to provide further data in the form of rankings and
ratings to each of the persons in the groups which they had
been studying. The various personality traits, as units, which
they had used in studying the personality as a whole, for the
first estimates, plus a variety of traits selected on the basis
of various theoretical considerations, were used as the basis
for this further study. Not until all rankings and ratings were
complete were the results of the first correlations made known
to the two raters. Indices were computed to describe the relationship between the actual tolerance rank and the specific
trait rankings. Since the traits were only casually defined and
not systematically selected, there is little point in reproduc-
ing all of the findings here. This analysis was considered preliminary and the more critically controlled study will be reported below.

On the basis of the correlation of tolerance rank derived
from the attitude test and the trait ranks assigned from study
of personality sketches, the preliminary hypotheses were that
tolerance is positively correlated with introversion, negatively
correlated with outgoingness; and positively correlated with
self-confidence, intolerance being associated with lesser degrees of self-confidence.

The More Intensive Study

In another sample an attempt was made to measure the relationship between tolerance and the specific traits indicated
more quantitatively and objectively. In the C.C.N.Y.--Business
group performance on the Bernreuter Personality Inventory was

available. Measures of self-confidence and sociability were secured by scoring for each of the two Flanagan scales (4). The
correlation between the score on the F-1-C scale and tolerance
as measured by the mean social distance for thirty-two nations
and races gave as the coefficient r = -.20. This correlation
was based on 118 cases and has a standard error of .09. Within
the limitations of this qualification, it suggests that those
with more confidence in themselves tend to be more tolerant.
When the Bernreuter test is scored for sociability (F-2-S scale)
the scores are interpreted so that the higher the score the less
sociable is the individual. The correlation between general
tolerance and F-2-S score gives the coefficient r = .16 with a
standard error of .09. Within the limits imposed by the qualification of the coefficient by its standard error, the correlation suggests that the more gregarious individuals, as measured by this test, tend to be less tolerant.

Using the Bernreuter test as the only criterion with which to
measure personality traits involved seemed unwise. It is difficult to say precisely what the scores on the test mean in terms
of the social behavior of the individual. The correlations do
not conform to the requirements of conventionally accepted criteria for statistical significance, and it seemed desirable to
supplement this approach by a more careful, clinical analysis
of personality in relation to tolerance.

In the sample of thirty-four cases from C.C.N.Y.--Arts, from
whom personality sketches had been obtained as described at the
beginning of the chapter, the five most tolerant and five most
intolerant individuals were selected on the basis of their responses on the social distance test of attitude. The ten personality studies of these individuals served as the basis for
another series of studies. Their expressed tolerance for nations
and races on the social distance scale was not indicated in any
way on the case description, random identification numbers were
the only means of designating the individuals. These papers
were turned over to a clinical psychologist for analysis.* She
was given to understand that they represented a random selec-

---

*Ruth E. Hartley co-operated in these studies, preparing the
personality analyses reported in this chapter.

tion of ten sketches from the sample of C.C.N.Y.--Arts, and
that the analysis she was being asked to make was preliminary
to another series of studies, the purpose of which she did not
know.

After the ten cases had been carefully read, analyses were
made of each of the individuals in terms of whatever seemed of
greatest significance in the light of each personality rather
than of any predetermined schedule. After the first analysis of
each case, summaries were written. She was then asked to divide
the ten individuals, based upon her personality and charactero-
logical summaries, into dichotomies, into two classes of five
each on any systematic basis she could. As many dichotomies
could be undertaken as seemed reasonable in the light of the
personality summaries which had been prepared. The emphasis was
on finding bases for classifying the personalities into dichotomies. Finally, the clinician was told of the way in which the
cases had been selected, and was asked to sort them into high
and low tolerance categories based on a general estimate.

Statistical Considerations

In our analysis of the sortings made on the basis of personality, we shall attempt to analyse the correspondence between
the dichotomy with respect to personality variables, and the
dichotomy with respect to tolerance on the social distance test.
In sorting ten papers into two groups of five each, it is possible to make a total of 252 different arrangements (number of
combinations of ten items taken in groups of five). Using for-
mulae for computing the number of combinations that can be made
in selecting differently constituted groups of five from a sample of ten, we can estimate the probabilities associated with
any particular relationship which may be observed. Thus selection on a chance basis would result in putting five of category
A in class C and five of category B in class D, once in 252
times. The probability of getting five of category A in either
class C or D and necessarily the five of category B in D or C,
would be two in 252, $p = .00794$. Concerning the probability of
getting four from one of the original categories in any one of
the new dichotomies the following line of reasoning would apply.

There are five different ways of getting combinations of four items from a sample of five units. Thus, we might expect among the 252 possible combinations, five different ones which would include some groupings of four from class A. Associated with each of these five different ways of getting four there might be any one of the five items from class B. This represents a total of twenty-five different combinations in 252 in which any four members of class A could be expected to occur in class C. To estimate the probability of finding four from class A in either C or D, we multiply this by two so that we might expect to find groupings of four from one of the original categories in some one of the new dichotomies by chance alone fifty times in 252 sortings or an equivalent of $p = .198$. Table XIV gives the fuller statement of the number of times we might expect to get different numbers of units from, let us say, class A of an original dichotomy in class C of a second sorting.

TABLE XIV

Analysis of Chance Distributions of Combinations of Ten Papers
Sorted into Two Groups of Five Each in Terms of Frequency
of Combinations that Might Be Expected to Contain Dif-
ferent Numbers of Papers from One of the Original
Dichotomies (e.g., the "high" tolerance group)

Number from the Original Category in the Combination	Frequency of Occurrence by Chance
5A	1
4A (-1B)	25
3A (-2B)	100
2A (-3B)	100
1A (-4B)	25
0A (-5B)	1
	252

The Correspondence in the Sortings

The very last personality sortings made in the series undertaken is worth mentioning first. This was an attempt to estimate general tolerance, first from the personality summaries,
and then from the fuller case descriptions. Since the analyses
were in terms of definitely labeled C and D categories, the
single expression rather than the doubling would more correctly
express the theoretical chance possibilities in the correspondence with the original dichotomy. Both sortings proved identi-
cal, although they were independently done and there was no
conscious memory during the second of the results of the first.
The results showed that four of the five were correctly placed
in each of the two dichotomies. Only one pair of individuals
was misplaced, and these same two were misplaced both times.
The possibility of getting this result or better by chance is
26/252 (see Table XIII). This seems to confirm the conclusion
suggested earlier that tolerance can be estimated from the total personality picture of the individual. It is interesting to
note that the pair of case histories which were confused in
their placement were the only two in the ten where the students
had not followed the outline as it was offered. In length, these
two were only six pages each (standard double space typewritten
pages directly comparable to all the others), while the other
outlines, when typed up, were respectively 10, 11, 12, 12, 13,
15, 22, and 40 pages long.

The analyses of the case outlines in this study were undertaken chiefly in accordance with the outline of personality
suggested by Murray (13).

As described above, without reference to the factor of tolerance, a number of variables were selected as criteria for dividing the cases into two groups. Of those selected, later
analysis revealed that the following variables did not seem related to tolerance. These variables, when the cases were sorted,
included within each unit of the dichotomy on personality characteristics, combinations of three and two from the two groups
divided on tolerance: inferiority feelings, feelings of having
been cheated, repressed aggression, super-ego conflict, projectivity, and integration of ego ideal.

Two classification schemes coincided with the original dichotomy to the extent of having within each of the new categories
four of the five in the tolerance dichotomies. These two classification schemes were based on (1) the quality of the need for
achievement and (2) a combination of intraception (interest in
imaginative activities) and endocathection (preoccupation with
inner processes). Our discussion of methodology in this sorting
suggests that this degree of correspondence might be expected
fifty-two times in 252 sortings on a chance basis. The relationship is therefore not such as to preclude an explanation on the
basis of chance. However, it seems sufficiently interesting to
make it worth while accepting the existence of the relationships as tentative hypotheses pending further research.

The hypothesis suggests that the tolerant individuals have
high need for achievement. They seem to have a strong need

to accomplish something difficult. To master, manipulate or
organize physical objects, human beings, or ideas. To do
this as rapidly, and as independently as possible. To overcome obstacles and attain a high standard. To excel one's
self. To rival and surpass others. To increase self-regard
by the successful exercise of talent (13, p.164).

To make intense, prolonged and repeated efforts to accomplish something difficult. To work with singleness of purpose
towards a high and distant goal. To have the determination to
win. To try to do everything well. To be stimulated to excel
by the presence of others, to enjoy competition. To exert
will power; to overcome boredom and fatigue (13, p.164).

For the intolerant group we find this characteristic rather low.

There seems to be a tendency for the individuals at the tolerant extreme to be interested in imaginative activity and pre-
occupied with inner processes. These individuals tend to have
"an imaginative, subjective human outlook," (p. 747) -- "a preoccupation with inner activities: feelings, fantasies, generalizations, theoretical reflections, artistic conceptions, religious studies" (p. 745). The intolerant people have an "occupation with outer events" (p. 746) -- with an "enjoyment of
clearly observable results. A tangible mechanical outlook"
(p. 746). These two empirical findings warrant further test before they can be accepted for generalization; particular effort
should be made to test other types of samples.

For further orientation, after the clinical psychologist had made all of the individual personality and character sketches for the ten individuals and all (and more than all) the categorizations which she felt were warranted, the true position in the tolerance dichotomy of each of the cases was designated. The task was then to attempt to formulate some general characteristics of the tolerant and intolerant personalities. Here we would expect to find the intrusion of possible halo factors in the summaries by the clinician. These summaries are not to be taken as final objective analyses, but rather as cues for further work. The analyses, however, have some merit, since all of the individual outlines had been interpreted and summarized before the observer was notified of the tolerance aspect of the cases and consequently the halo error may be presumed to have been reduced to a minimum though projection of the theoretical biases of the observer may have influenced the results.

The relatively tolerant personality in this type of collegiate sample is likely to exhibit some combination of the following characteristics: a strong desire for personal autonomy associated with a lack of need for dominance, a strong need for friendliness, along with a personal seclusiveness, fear of competition, a tendency to placate others along with lack of general conformity to the mores. He is likely to be fairly serious, to be interested in current events, to have ideas about bettering society, to be a member of a political group and to have great need for personal achievement in the vocational area. He is likely to be an accepting personality, disliking violence, able to appreciate the contributions of others, conscious of feeling that people tend to be more or less alike and adopting a nurturant rather than a dominant attitude toward those younger than he. He is conscious of conflicts concerning loyalties and duties, and thinks very seriously about moral questions. His interests center about what are commonly called the social studies, reading and journalism. Although personally seclusive, he has a great need to be socially useful.

The relatively intolerant personality might be expected to combine in varying degrees the following characteristics: unwillingness to accept responsibility, acceptance of conventional mores, a rejection of "serious" groups, rejection of political interests and desire for groups formed for purely social purposes, absorption with pleasure activities, a conscious conflict between play and work, emotionality rather than rationality, ex-

treme egocentrism, interest in physical activity, the body,
health. He is likely to dislike agitators, radicals, pessimists.
He is relatively uncreative, apparently unable to deal with
anxieties except by fleeing from them. Often his physical activity has in it a compulsive component; it may be that this
compulsion to be on the move, that is, constantly occupied with
sports, motoring, traveling, etc. serves for him the same function that study and activities with social significance serve
in the case of the individual with high tolerance. Both the
tolerant and intolerant individuals have anxieties, but there
seems to be a distinct difference in the way in which they work
them out.

Such characteristics as projectivity, distrust of people,
feelings of inferiority, feelings of not belonging, and personal seclusiveness, seem to break across these tolerance categories. Two tolerant individuals who seemed to share a good
many characteristics with the intolerant group had what was apparently a firmly crystallized code which did not permit of in-
equality in tolerance of groups, although one of these was
freely rejective of peers, parents, and other individuals on an
individual basis. While it is true that such a code also appears
in the case of one individual correctly judged to have low tolerance, it is so overshadowed by superficiality, banality, obvious need for dominance, emotionality, insincerity, unwillingness to accept responsibility, and need for conformity that it
seems to exert no real influence. What one might call infantilism is especially marked in the intolerant group. One individual
who from a superficial examination does not otherwise seem to
belong with this group, depends on cliches for his value organization of life; that is, he accepts morals pointed in plays
and books at their face value with apparently little understanding of a realistic sort. This was one of the individuals incor-
rectly placed at first, before the significance of such dependence was fully recognized.

The above suggestions by no means represent conclusive reports
of the differentiation between tolerant and intolerant personalities. They are offered solely as hypotheses based upon the
studies conducted. It must be emphasized again that the particular sample analyzed represented extremes from a group of students who are originally selected for very high intelligence
for admission to college, and represent a group which in comparison with other schools studied is very tolerant. It must be
remembered also that many of these students are themselves members of discriminated-against minorities.

To supplement these hypotheses, we are including reports by
two of the tolerant students and two of the intolerant students,
together with analytical notes. The first two cases, 26 and 19,
are at the intolerant extreme; cases 32 and 28 represent the
high tolerance group.

Subject #26

This is the first time that I have ever been called upon to
analyze myself, and I must confess that I hardly know where to
begin. When I really come to think of it, I don't believe that
I know myself much better than anybody else does. Of course, I
know my likes and dislikes, but I never took the pains to in-
quire into the whys and wherefores of my likes and dislikes. As
to my aptitudes, I frankly confess that I don't know if I'm
better at one thing than I am at another, with the possible exception of mathematics. I know that I'm definitely not mathe-
matically inclined. Generally speaking, though, I've found that
I'm good at most anything I tackle. And I try to steer clear of
tackling anything as much as I possibly can. I'll admit it right
now, before I go any further. I am lazy, but what I mean lazy!
In school, outside of school, at home, away from home, wherever
I may be, I invariably look for some way out of doing anything
constructive, preferring to loaf my time away.

As to my skills, I repeat I find myself quite apt at anything
I undertake. I've never undertaken anything requiring much
skill, so I can't say that I'm more skillful at this than I am
at that. In school I do know that I'm more skillful in memory
work than I am in some other sort of task. At home, I'm not
much use about the house, but I can take an automobile engine
apart and put it together again, and the car will still run. By
the way, that's one of the greatest pleasures I derive out of
my leisure time activities which are very circumscribed. I honestly enjoy motoring. I detest driving in the city. But give me
a car on the country roads, and boy oh boy! Incidentally, I
spend most of my leisure time thus. I find it rather expensive,
but I feel it's worth it. I only need one person to keep me
company in the car, and a radio, and boy, watch my smoke.

The things that I find most unpleasant invariably occur in
school. For, at home, and in my leisure time I avoid them as
much as I possibly can. To be specific, I hate to do research
work. It's so cut and dried and such a routine matter that I
cannot manage to keep my attention centered upon the task before me. I virtually copy everything for fear of omitting something of importance. Be that as it may, I know that I simply
must force myself to go into the library when I have to do some

research, especially when the weather becomes balmy and the
thermometer begins to spurt. Speaking of balmy weather and ris-
ing thermometers, the thing I enjoy most doing is to get out of
New York City when the summer rolls around.

I would like very much to throw up school and go to live upstate, but evidentally my family has other plans for me. They
claim that there is nothing to be made in farming, and maybe
they are right. At any rate, I would certainly enjoy leaving
the city and spending some time upstate.

Perhaps one reason for my desire to leave the city is my seem-
ing distrust for people. I honestly cannot account for it. All
I know is that when I meet a new personality, I am instantly on
the defensive, becoming somewhat of a boor, as a young lady
once referred to me. I never become intimate with a person I've
just met, and sometimes it's a matter of years before I thaw
out and really become friendly. But once I do become intimate
with someone, I'd go out of my way to do anything for him. That
is because I don't make friends very easily, and when I do accept somebody as a friend, he is usually "all right." When I
was a youngster, I lived in one neighborhood for 13 years and
had a pack of friends. I moved when I was going on my 14th year,
and I can truthfully say that for the next two or three years,
I was miserable. I didn't have one real friend. I guess I was
too picky, but I reasoned that since I am looking for a friend,
I want somebody that I can really look upon as a friend. I found
him and several others after about 2-3 years. In the meantime,
I used to amuse myself, hardly ever going out, even to play ball
or such with the kids of my age. I preferred going around with
the grown ups. That is why I grew up too early. Today, I am only
19 years of age, yet I feel like 23 and have been taken for such
by many people. I don't seem to have any patience for 19 year
old boys, a finding which sometimes fills me with fear. I am
growing old before my time, and I am missing most of my youth.

To get back to the question before me, I repeat that I am not
at all spontaneous in my relations with others. With those that
I have something in common, I am more or less drawn out and I'll
show them every sign of friendliness. But with those that I have
only a nodding acquaintance, or a "Hello-how-are-you--goodbye"
acquaintance, I am very reserved, holding back (consciously) as
much as possible, never making the first move toward becoming
better acquainted. Why? I don't know. Maybe it is just that I
was born with a suspicious nature, or maybe it's just that I'm
an unfriendly sort, that I don't want to make friends. But I'm
not an unfriendly soul, and I do want to make friends. Then why
do I act thus? Perhaps I'm a psychological case.

I am most free when I am by myself. In fact, I am free only

when I am by myself, except when I am in the presence of my cousin. I was raised together with my cousin, although she is a bit older than I am; she is my sole confidante -- I tell her things that I don't tell my own parents, but of course I don't tell her everything. It's very significant that my group of friends always stick together. We always stick together and we always go out together. It's very seldom that we allow any outsider to join us. Not that we are independent or anything like that. It's just that we know each other, what we are, and we don't want any intrusions upon our friendship. The only thing that I don't like about my friends is that no one of them has a mind of his own. If there are any decisions to be made, I make them all. And the rest follow me blindly. Either they have faith in me, or they don't care one way or the other. That's why we get along so well.

Don't get the impression that I only know people that I like. I also know many people that I dislike, whom I avoid as much as possible. In fact, I might say that I cross the street sometimes to avoid meeting them. I can recall about a half-dozen of them offhand. One I can't stand because he loses all decorum in a situation calling for a display of dignity. A second because he is a loud-mouth, a "wise guy." A third I don't like because his conduct is unbecoming a gentleman -- he forgets his manners and has a habit of becoming inebriated when the occasion least calls for it. A fourth (a young lady) I absolutely detest because of her high ideas -- she insists on going out to the biggest and most expensive places on my college-boy allowance -- in short, a "gold digger." A fifth (another young lady) I just can't stand because she looks upon me as a kid when I want everybody to look upon me as a young man. She prefers them 23 and 24 and even 25. The sixth I really have it in for (although my sense of fair play tells me that I'm not being fair) because she up and told me what she thinks of me after I told her up and down just what I thought of her.

My reaction to those younger than myself I have already explained. I get great enjoyment of looking down on them, and take pleasure in humoring them. Towards my younger sister and her girl friends I feel quite the "big brother." I get an awful kick out of the way she respects me, and in appreciation of awareness of my rank, I slip her a quarter now and then. I'm quite a modest chap, so when my sister's friends (who think a great deal of me) start the "oo," "oh," and "ah," it makes me feel pretty good.

I carry on the same way when I am watching a circus. The antics of the performers hand me as big a kick as they do a child of 10. I can say the same when I see in the movies some such

scenes as "Our Gang Comedy," "Popeye," etc. And when I see a
group of youngsters playing "hide-and-seek" or a game of sand-
lot football, it is all I can do to keep from jumping in the
fun.

Similarly, I feel old when I am in the presence of the things
that make me feel young again, for they make me aware of the
fact that I am no longer a youngster, but well on the way to
adulthood. This may sound paradoxical, but it is so just the
same. In addition, my attendance at college makes me aware of
the fact that I have grown up; the realization that I will soon
graduate from college and have to assume the responsibilities
that every young job-seeker labors under; the realization that
now I have more expenses than ever which means that I will soon
have to assume financial responsibilities, a thing that never
troubled me when I was younger. All these conditions make me
aware of the fact that I am growing up, and make me feel quite
old. Sometimes I feel frightened when I realize that I am getting older, a feeling which I am sure many of my associates
share with me.

Frankly speaking, I feel at home only when I am alone or with
someone that I am intimate with, one who understands me and
whom I understand. Into this category would fall only my immedi-
ate friends. Of course, I am made to feel at home more or less
when I visit people or places or see things that I am accus-
tomed to visiting and seeing. For example, it wouldn't be fair
to say that I don't feel at home, or I don't feel that I belong
to the school that I attend, more particularly the classes of
which I am a member. I do have a sense of comfort and a feeling
of belonging when I sit in any class in school or have occasion
to refer to the library or any other department of the University. But it definitely is not a sense of belonging to the same
degree as when I sit at the dinner table in the evening with
the rest of my family, or when I go to visit somebody that I
know very well. It is all a matter of degree. For that matter,
I can say the same about any club or organization that I may be
fortunate enough to be connected with. If I am in the organization for a long time, know everybody in the club, and am taking
an active part in formulating its policies and in their execu-
tion, I certainly feel at home when I attend their meetings and
affairs. And when I look about me and see all the familiar faces
with recognition in their eyes, and I see the familiar sights
that I expect to see and hear, then I feel that I do belong
here, that I am connected with this group, whether it be an economic group, a political group, or a religious group, or a social organization. This is my organization and I belong here. It
is a grand feeling to look about you and think "This is where I

belong. This is where my interests are wrapped up. This is
where everybody takes an interest in me, where everyone regards
me as a brother and I regard them likewise. This is where I
spend some of the most delightful hours of my life. This is
where I want to devote all my time. This is my group, and I want
to do everything possible to better it, to further its cause
and thus increase its value and its benefits. How glad I am to
belong here."

Please do not get the impression that I feel that I belong to
everything I come across. Far from it. As I have already had
occasion to mention, I am very hard to please, but once I do
join up and become identified with something or other, it is
usually worth my while and the time I put into it. For instance,
I am identified with my family and friends, with my school, with
social, political, and religious organizations, with my neighborhood, -- in fact with anything local. By that I mean anything
that surrounds me in the pursuance of my life and which I come
into contact time and again. But that is as far as it goes. Beyond the few activities that circumscribe my life, I do not
necessarily feel identified with any groups or activities, with
the possible exception of one, and that is the United States of
America. When I hear mentioned the United States, I feel a definite sense of belonging, that I am one of the more than 130,-
000,000 people that reside in the U.S. and are thankful to be
thus privileged, especially in the face of existing conditions;
proud that the United States, to which I belong, is the best
country in the world, glad to be able to enjoy its advantages
and privileges, proud to be able to say that I am an American.

I only know that I and the people with whom I have come into
contact think only in terms of localism, that we belong only to
those groups or activities of which we can easily conceive and
with a minimum of effort.

Truthfully, I am never too confident of myself. But, like
everybody else, I do have some confidence in myself. I have confidence in myself in most everything I undertake (with the possible exception of the Biology practicum I just underwent). When
you speak of this or that, and you say this or that, or you
think so and so about so and so, people are inclined to answer:
"Oh yeah? Well, don't be so smart about this or that. It's not
as easy as all that." What we mean for self-confidence they take
as arrogance or so much talk. They come back with "Actions speak
louder than words."

As I have already said, I too have some confidence in myself.
I usually find myself able to cope with anything that I have
undertaken, or anything that has cropped up, even if unexpected-
ly. At least, so it has been in the past, which has served to

increase confidence in myself. I have confidence in myself when
I enroll in any course in the school or take a test in any
course, or anything that I may undertake in or out of the house.
Of course, this confidence of mine does not apply to everything. For instance, I don't for one moment have the idea that
I can take apart an automobile engine and put it together again
so that it will run. I do have confidence enough to tinker
around with it, and although I do know quite a bit about a motor, still I don't have enough confidence in myself to take it
apart for fear that I may not be able to put it together again.
But as far as running an automobile goes, I believe I can hold
my own against the average driver. I'll drive anything that has
four wheels and a motor, and that is no idle boast. I have
driven everything in the passenger car line from an old Model T
Ford to a high-powered 12 cylinder Lincoln, and almost everything from a Diesel engine road tractor to an International
3-ton truck. This may all sound like so much idle chatter, but
I would never have brought this up except to prove my point.

Although I started off this section by saying that I do not
have too much confidence in myself, I still maintain I really
don't with the exception of the things I have just mentioned.
But the arguments I have presented have covered a good deal of
ground, after all. So maybe I underestimate myself when I say
that I don't have much confidence in myself. It seems that I
have as much self-confidence as has anybody else. And in view
of my past experiences, I think this attitude is well-founded,
it at all founded.

Notwithstanding all this, with my self-confidence and all,
there still are fears that pervade my soul. The only way I can
account for them is to attribute them to human nature. This
sounds like a rather lame excuse or apology for something, but,
really, that's the only way I can account for them. The fear of
dark I have long since overcome. So, too, with the fear of
superstition. But there are several fears from which I still
suffer, some rather violently. One of these is a fear of close
spaces, claustrophobia.

Another fear I suffer from is a fear of high places. I have
lived a good deal of my life on high floors, but I have never
been able to conquer this fear. I have fallen and been thrown
off high places, was several times injured thus, once seriously
when I was pushed off a stone wall 10-12 feet high and put a
hole in the sidewalk with my head, the scar of which I bear
around with me, which has only served to increase my fear of
high places. This fear of the 12-foot fence I overcame in later
years, even to the extent of deliberately jumping off it to
prove to myself that I was not afraid.

Finally, I am afraid of old age. Not afraid of death, mind you, but old age. When I see the helplessness of old age and the senility and crankiness, I begin to wish that I don't live long enough to become old. I am not afraid of death. I don't even give it a second thought. Only the good die young.

In most every decision I make, the decision one or another is a result of an inner conflict, two opposing forces, one tending to pull me one way and the other trying to influence my decision in the opposite direction. This is a characteristic of my line of thought and the thinking of everybody else.

I can think back to my childhood days, when I used to have real inner conflicts. I used to be quite a kid in my day. One force would urge me to swipe that cigarette from my father's pack of cigarettes because all the other kids were smoking and why shouldn't I and besides it made me grow up quicker if I smoked, while another force said: "Don't you do it. You know what will happen if you get caught doing it." But I did it just the same. Similarly, come Saturday morning, I used to go to the movies with all the kids of the neighborhood. But I would always manage to raise my mother's ire on Friday night, with the result that: "No movies for you tomorrow, young man, until you apologize for your actions." Of course, I wouldn't apologize. Wasn't I in the right? Didn't I know what I wanted? On Saturday morning when my movie money wasn't forthcoming, I began to realize that maybe I was in the wrong, and that I owed my mother an apology. But my childish pride wouldn't let me. I wanted to go to the movies so badly that day. They were featuring Buck Jones, and such. Something urged me to apologize, yet my pride wouldn't let me. I was going to get even with my mother. I was going to show her that I had pride too. I don't have to tell you what it is like. Every boy and girl has gone through it at one time or another. I would start to sulk, and that is where the beating of my life came in. In all seems very foolish when I look back upon it now, and I have to laugh at my childish antics, but at that time I was very serious about it. Why, it was almost a matter of life and death. At least, so it seemed to me. And it was all a result of a ridiculous childish pride. Hang it all, children shouldn't have a pride. At least not to the extent where they would cut off their noses to spite their faces.

I have never been given much to thinking about Heaven, for I don't believe in life after death. Nor for that matter, although it may show utter lack of diplomacy to say so, do I believe in God. It is my contention that were there a God, he would have manifested himself long ago, and in view of the war conditions of the world today, with all its suffering, and the persecution of the innocent and the helpless, if God has done nothing to

put an end to it, then I am forced to conclude that there is no
God. Surely, if he allows madmen and gangsters to continue to
cause so much suffering among the innocent and helpless, a thing
which they themselves do not believe but use it much as one
would use the Red scare to fool their people to continue them
in power, then how can I believe, much as I may like to, that
there is an All-powerful and All-Mighty, the one who created
and even today oversees everything. Surely, if there were a God,
he would put a stop to these abominable goings-on and punish
the persecutors, and alleviate the sufferings of the wretched
and persecuted. But since I am asked to develop a picture of
life after death, Heaven, I must call upon my imagination to
supply me with such details as may be necessary in the painting
of that portrait.

I rather picture Heaven as a sort of Utopia, a place where
there is no wanting nor any suffering nor any oppression. Everybody is free to do as he or she pleases. There are no moral
codes, for these people do not have to be told what to do and
what not to do. They already know what is right and what is not
right. Is it not true that only righteous people can even hope
of entering Heaven? There is no working for a living in Heaven.
As a result, there are no privileged in Heaven, except those as
may be necessary to the preservation of peace in Heaven, to ad-
just all misunderstandings which may arise among the residents
in Heaven, and to procure the necessities and luxuries of life
for the inhabitants. Literally, it is a place where one just
has to walk in the street to find gold, except that there is no
gold in Heaven since money is of no consequence there, there
being nothing to sell or buy everything being free, no charge,
gratis, yours for the taking. In this land are found the most
fertile and rich food-bearing trees with the most luscious and
widest assortment of fruits that can be conceived. If one is
hungry, all one has to do is to pluck the fruit from the tree.
I haven't worked out a method of getting steaks and pork chops,
for there is to be no killing in Heaven, not even a cow or a
pig. I guess that in my Heaven the inhabitants will have to become vegetarians. I would even charge exorbitant rents to discourage people from coming to my Heaven.

Seriously though, if I were pinned down and commanded to
write my impression of Heaven, I would picture a true Utopia,
such as Sir Thomas More pictured. I could picture a communal
life, with no private ownership of wealth, everybody rather doing all he could to advance Heaven and at the same time reaping
the benefits of his work and the work of the others collective-
ly. Of course, there would have to be some group of individuals
to represent everybody and oversee everything and everybody and

see that no one exceeded the code of ethics. All ownership
would be communal, as would be production and distribution. The
inhabitants would be enjoying the luxuries denied them on earth,
varying with the length of time that you live in Heaven and the
amount of good you have done for the community. The most privileged and luxury-loving would be the oldest inhabitants and
those who have done most toward bettering the lot of his neigh-
bor and his community. All newcomers would have just the bar-
est necessities and no privileges until he proved his worth by
working for the community. So that in the end all would be
equal, for the now-privileged also were newcomers at one time.

Quite unlike the preceding section, herein I am called back
to earth with its worries and problems that cause anxiety and
make one feel upset. I need look no further than school to find
examples and instances of tension-producing, upsetting moments.
Almost any test is bound to introduce tension to the subject
and cause him to become violently upset, especially if one is
unprepared for the examination. Even if one is prepared for the
test, he is under a strain, though I don't know why. Speaking
for myself, I can recall back to my high school days, when I
had to take the State Regents Examination, I remember how I used
to go into the examination room all atremble, when just a week
prior to that examination I had taken a test in the subject,
covering the same material, and had emerged with flying colors.
When the papers were distributed, I was so frightened that my
head began swimming around and.I couldn't see what was printed
on the paper before me. I immediately was taken violently ill
and had to leave the room, and I was unable to do anything for
the remainder of that day, nor the next either from brooding
over my performance.

I remember another incident that sent my blood-pressure soar-
ing way up to the upper levels. I had been recommended to
Arthur Murray Dancing School as a dancing instructor. I had confidence in my ability to dance. I have done enough of it to have
confidence. Yet, when I got on the dance floor, my heart was
pumping to beat the band, and when the young lady I was dancing
with made a comment or asked me a question, I was too choked up
to answer coherently. This palpitation of the heart seems to be
a habit with me. I am very unstable in that respect. That hap-
pens every time I go to see a doctor. I am as sound as a bear,
yet every time ·I go to see a doctor, my heart begins to race
against its own beat.

At no time can we say that we run our lives as we please. From
infancy on, the pattern of our lives is already cut out for us.
Why, even when we reach adulthood, we still do not decide the
course our lives are to follow. Either directly or indirectly,

there are certain influences, moral, cultural, religious, political, economic, social, that bring great pressure to bear on
our thoughts and actions. Our mode of life is cut out for us by
our predecessors, and we must either conform or sink. This is
felt even more so by the present young generation, for whom
there seems to be no hope of there ever being any opportunity
for individuality. Why, it is all the present generation can do
to stay afloat, even by conformity. I am no anarchist but I do
contend that there will have to take place a violent upheaval
in some phase of our society (I'm rather inclined to think it
is the economic phase) before we young ones will have a chance
to show some originality and really start living.

Let me show you what I mean by referring to my own, rather un-
eventful life. From infancy on, my life was cut out for me (at
least until I reached the age of 21). I lived the life led by
all the other people, eating, sleeping, and going to school. I
am still doing the same. Well, that is to be expected. But I
had rather hoped that when I finished school, I would then be
able to begin to earn money and live my own life. But evidently
society has other plans. My caste and position in life were predetermined even before I was born. Don't misunderstand me, I am
not a fatalist at heart. But circumstances would make it seem
as if fate had a hand in it. I can't rise out of my caste, for
all the avenues of escape in the direction of improvement have
long since been closed. No longer is there equal opportunity
for all.

I really shouldn't kick though. There is much more opportunity for individuality in my life than there is in the life led
by the son of a Rockefeller, for example. All his activities
are selected for him, and in his future station, though a secure one, is also not of his choosing. Sometimes I feel sorry
for such people. All their activities are rigidly classified
into "must" and "must not." This they must do and this they
must not do. This class of people they may associate with and
that type they may not. No such rigid classification for me. If
I feel like doing something (within reason, of course) I do it,
and no questions asked. I merely classify people into those
whom I want to associate with and those whom I don't like. There
is no must not see or talk to somebody about it. If I like
somebody, I'll see him if his father is serving a term at El-
mira or if his father is a big financier or industrialist. In
that respect, I have more than does the son of a Rockefeller. I
can still choose my friends. He cannot. His friends are chosen
for him by his parents.

On the whole, though, I don't think life is so bad. There
still are some nice things and some nice people left. I have

friends that I can turn to, and as long as there is some hope
left in the old boy, maybe things won't turn out so bad after
all.

Tolerance Analysis: Case 26

Among criteria for degrees of tolerance to be expected from
given subjects, the following kinds of indicators have usually
been available to us in their statements about themselves:

1. Specific information on attitudes or opinions that might
   be connected with tolerance for ethnic groups, such as
   political beliefs, or economic views.
2. Tendencies to accept or reject conventions of the common
   culture, of which we assume intolerance to be an accepted
   characteristic.
3. Personality needs that might be served by rejection or
   affiliation with others.

In the document submitted by Subject 26, we find some factors
that might indicate a high degree of tolerance: i.e., expressed
sympathy for the persecuted in general, an implied belief in
the economic basis for human happiness (indicating some rebellion against the common culture), a. vision of a communal heaven,
and membership in a group which is culturally subordinate. In a
document which is extraordinarily long, however, reference to
these items occupy a very small fraction of space.

On the other hand, we have many more items which would suggest a low degree of tolerance. Among these items, we have some
for each of the three categories suggested above. Among the
specific attitudes which might influence the subject's reaction
to ethnic groups, we find a special attachment to that which is
"local" and familiar, familiarity carrying a high positive emotional charge for him. Groups other than his own would automatically fall into the "unfamiliar," hence disliked, category.
He shows also an uncritical acceptance of conventional patrio-
tism, stresses the desirability of nationalistic views, and
"human nature" beliefs, with emphasis on hereditarian rather
than environmental explanations of behavior. This unquestioning
acceptance of these particular ready-made views would facili-
tate also the acceptance of national stereotypes, categoriza-

tion of individuals by ethnic group membership, and conventional valuation of different ethnic groups.

In the group of personality indicators, we find egocentricity and seclusiveness, making for superficiality in relations with others. He values people only for what they can give him. The needs to dominate his peers and to reject them are also present, preventing the formation of genuinely warm and friendly bonds. He indicates strong negative feelings towards his parents, along with great dependence on them. This combination of incompatible attitudes forces him to seek disguised channels for release of the tensions caused by his hostile feelings, which he cannot express directly towards their·original objects. Since he fears even to acknowledge his own aggressive impulses, he is driven to project them, making for a suspicious and belligerent approach to people. He has no capacity for sympathy or identification with his peers, apparently seeing in them only threats to himself.

This subject's general infantilism and dependence on his elders, along with his rigidity and love for the familiar, would make us expect him to accept all parts of the mores without question. When in addition the social code fulfills his personal needs for domination and aggression while freeing him of personal responsibility for their expression, it is inevitable that he should show a prevailing picture of low tolerance.

Subject #19

I

In school I should say that I am good at ·languages. In four terms of Latin at college I received three A's and one B. And in the subject of French, I received an A, B, and C.in three courses of the subject.

Outside of school, I consider myself to be a better than average runner. I do no running now. But 2 or 3 years ago I won a few medals for running.

In school, I find that I am poor in such subjects as history, or economics, etc. For no apparent reason I cannot become interested in these types of subjects. Lack of interest more than anything else, is, I think, responsible for the fact that I am poor in this type of subject. However, I also find myself to be poor in a different subject from those mentioned namely, English. One factor contributing to my poorness in this subject is that in the last four or five years I have done, I think, comparatively very little reading.

There are a number of things that I like to do. First of all, I like to participate in various sports. I like to play very much indoor baseball. I also like to play "association" a great deal, this game being played with a football. I also enjoy listening to the radio a great deal. I listen particularly to the radio programs of comedians. My favorite comedians are Jack Benny and Fred Allen. I go to the movies quite frequently. I also get quite a kick out of following up my sports. I am particularly interested in professional baseball, and football. I have my favorite team in each of these sports.

There are many things that I find unpleasant. One of these is doing school homework. In fact, if I am not making too great an admission, I find it actually unpleasant to go to college. Of course, I can't at all blame this on the college itself. The reason for this is that I have no hope at all for the future. Life to me is simply a daily grind with no future to.it, for me anyhow. This feeling toward college, is, as I see it, caused by my general outlook on life, since seeing nothing for the future, I consider myself to be wasting my time in college. Then the question is, why am I continuing to go to college if I don't desire to. The reasons, as I see it, are twofold. First and most important, my parents wouldn't give me a moment of rest, I know, if I left college. The reason for this is that they think I can make something of myself by going thru college. However, with my present outlook on life, of which my parents are unaware, I don't think that this is very possible. Then again, if I leave college I have to think of what I am going to do. Most naturally I would have to go to work. And since there aren't many jobs today it wouldn't be very easy to find one. Aware of this fact, but keeping in mind first and foremost the desires of my parents, I continue going to college. Another reason which contributes to a great deal of my lack of enjoyment is the fact that I feel intellectually inferior to many other people. This in fact is another reason why I find college unpleasant. This feeling of intellectual inferiority is tied up with my general inferiority, which I shall discuss in a later question

With those associates with whom I am really intimate, I should say that I am quite spontaneous. I should also say that I hold back a great deal with those with whom I am not very intimate. As far as girls are concerned, all I can say is that I don't associate with girls, but I think I can safely say that if I did there would be very little spontaneity in my relations with them. I feel most free when I am in the company of my intimate friends. I feel less free when I am in the company of people I

know but who are not intimate friends of mine. I feel least
free and very much so in the company of people who are total
strangers to me. I have only a few intimate friends. The name
of one is Paul Smith, and the names of the other two are John
Brown and Tom Jones. All three go to my college. I used to play
ball with John and Tom in the park in my district. In this way
I came to know them. We formed a club and Paul who already knew
the other two also joined the club. And it was there that I
came to know him. I like my intimate friends because I find
them to be people I can talk to frankly. When I have a problem
I can talk to them freely about it and get their assistance. I
feel quite safe in confiding to them. There are certain people
I dislike. There is one fellow who strikes me as being the
show-off type. He is always trying to attract attention to himself. There is another fellow I know whom I dislike. This fellow rarely gives credit when credit is due. He himself strikes
me as being a brilliant and capable fellow, yet when there is
some action which undoubtedly deserves praise he doesn't give
any or he is very reluctant to give it. This same fellow I find,
very readily offers adverse criticism. I wouldn't particularly
like to know him better. Then there is another fellow, who it
seems to me speaks in a manner which is artificial and assumed.
I certainly wouldn't care to be on more intimate terms with
this fellow.

III

My general reaction to those slightly younger than I is one
of feeling just about on a par with. What I mean to say is that
I feel more at ease and more comfortable in the presence of
slightly younger people than myself than I do in the presence
of slightly older persons. In the presence of people who are
slightly older than myself, I feel uncomfortable, embarrassed
and uneasy. I feel that I am inferior to persons slightly older
than I or for that matter also to people who are just as old as
I. I consider myself an adolescent. But, I am only 18 years old
so that the fact that I consider myself an adolescent isn't, I
don't think, too significant. I should say that I am accepted
at the level I consider myself. Those with whom I associate are
about as old as or slightly younger than I, and therefore I can
act without fear at the level which I consider myself.

IV

There is no particular place where I can truthfully say I
feel at home. However I do feel at home when I'm with my intimate friends. I feel myself to be a member of the clique of my
friends. I also feel that I belong with fellows who are about
my age and who are of about the same intellectual ability as I.
I feel that I don't belong with groups older than I especially

if they are intellectually superior. I know that as a general
rule if I talk to a person older than I, I can't look the person straight in the face.

V

I am most confident of myself when I know that I have no need
for worry. For example, if in a game perhaps, I know that my
opposition is not equal to me, I feel confident of myself. I
also feel most confident of myself in the presence of intimate
friends. I feel confident when I am in the presence of people
whom I feel to be superior, whether in age or intellectually.

There are a number of fears that bother me. For one, I fear
criticism. If I know that I will be criticized for a certain
action, I try not to do that thing which will bring criticism.
I also fear for my health. My resistance is quite low and I am
bothered by quite frequent colds. I am also bothered by the
fact that I am shorter than average in stature. I am also
bothered by what to me is the fact that I am competing in college with students whom I consider more intelligent than I. All
these factors combine to make me a timid and sensitive person
and helps to give me a feeling of inferiority.

VI

There are a number of situations in which I have inner conflicts. For example, I have inner conflict when I think of the
question of college. I frequently feel to myself that college
will be of no use to me in the future and I wonder to myself
why I am going. But after all, now is not the time to overthrow
the work of two years, I just as soon think to myself. Then
again, I know that the chances of getting a job now, if I
weren't in college, would be very slim. However, my attitude
toward college is part of my general outlook toward life. My
outlook on life is one of resignation to whatever may come. I
frequently do things which cause my conscience to bother me. I
try to tell myself that what I did was right and still my conscience bothers me. This isn't so bad. What isn't so good is
the fact that my conscience seems to bother me very easily, more
so I imagine than an ordinary person's conscience bothers him.

I frequently have inner conflict, also, when I think of the
question of suicide. I feel many times that my life isn't worth
the trouble of living it and I think of committing suicide. However, I immediately see that I haven't the nerve to do so. Possibly the answer is that I am not disgusted enough with life to
leave it. Or to put it affirmatively, I still hope for the better. And I probably will never give up hoping and probably never
commit suicide, though I am making the mistake in saying never.

VII

I am happiest, from my point of view, when I can forget every-

thing, my troubles, and sorrows, etc. I should say that I am
happiest when I participate in sports and am active. As frequently as I can, I participate in various sports. If I had a
magic wishing wand, I think that I should ask for good health
for myself, my parents and brothers and sisters. I think that I
should hope to have, at present, good health rather than money,
because this I think would make a great change in my attitude
toward life.

As concerns the question of heaven, I must say that I have·
thought very little on the subject. The fact is, I don't think
I should say I firmly believe in heaven. As far as I can analyze myself, I am in grave doubt as to its existence. At the
same time, I am fearful lest there is a heaven. I should say
that an important reason for my doubt and uncertainty is the
fact that my life has turned out as it has. I frequently ask
myself the question whether it is possible that there really is
a Supreme Being and a Heaven, and if there is why doesn't he
help those who are in need of assistance, and in that category
I should include myself. I think I can safely say if the situation in which I find myself were not as it is, there shouldn't
be any or there would be very little doubt in my mind as to the
existence of a heaven. When I think of my shortcomings, faults,
my failures, etc. I find myself quite unhappy.

VIII

I frequently feel tense, anxious or upset. The most recent
situation in which I was anxious was the day after the last
basketball game which City College played. In the morning I
happened to remember that the varsity had played a game the
night before. And just as suddenly I became anxious because I
wanted to find out the results of the game. However, activity
soon removed the anxiety with the disappearance of the thought.
However, as soon as I thought of the game again, I again became
anxious. However, in this situation, I should say that though I
was upset, it was not very much. It seems that the least little
thing can create tension in me. For example, if I think of going
to the park to play ball I feel excited. I should say that the
reason for my being upset at the slightest thing is due to the
fact that there is a great deal of tension.

For me the fundamental organization seems to be to make myself succeed for my own benefit and to be socially useful.

From my point of view living is divided into a few categories:
1. nutrition; 2. propagating; 3. participating (in society).

I should classify things according to the value they possess.
In the first class would be the most valuable things. Then
would come the less valuable and the least valuable things.

I would classify people to intelligence. And I should class
them in three groups:
1. In the first group I should place the supernormal.
2. In the second group I should place the normal.
3. In the third group I should place the abnormal.

Tolerance Analysis: Case #19

Subject 19 seems to be very self-consistent, all indicators
pointing to a low degree of tolerance for members of ethnic
groups other than his own. He confesses to a complete lack of
social interests, suggesting the absence of any consciously organized code of behavior with reference to national groups. We
should, therefore, expect him to exhibit the attitudes common
to the community. He is, moreover, infantile, egocentric and
seclusive, unable to detach any libido from himself. Warmth of
understanding, sympathy for others or any emotionally charged
interest in them cannot be expected from him. Completely lacking in the capacity for overt rebellion, so dependent on parental help that he cannot risk parental sanctions, convinced of
his own inability to care for himself, this subject must blindly
follow the codes of his culture (in which, presumably, his parents also acquiesce).

In addition to these considerations, a socially acceptable
focus for negative feelings offers him one valuable channel for
release of tensions caused by the repression of almost all aggressive impulses. He cannot release such impulses except in
disguised forms, lest he lay himself open to criticism or pun-
ishment. The hierarchy of acceptance generally extended to different ethnic groups in this culture is of further value to
this subject because of his need to compensate for strong feelings of personal inferiority. He can safely channel his hates,
his resentments, his need to feel better than someone else without risking parental or social stricture, and he has no capacity
for that sympathy or identification that might trouble his
easily troubled "conscience." Culturally directed prejudices offer this subject the line of least risk and greatest satisfaction in directing hostility and obtaining psychological gratu-
ity.

Subject #32

I

In any discussion of an individual it is an essential thing
to know his background in order to explain his character. It is
therefore advisable to give, at the beginning, a brief outline
of my background which will be elaborated on as the report pro-
gresses.

My mother and father were both born in S----- and at the
early age of 13 or 14 began to work. Since that time both have
worked hard and on the whole had a none too comfortable life.
They had had no education, formal, that is, and believe that
education is probably one of the most important, if not the
most important, factors in determining the life of any person.
They therefore determined that their children, my brother and I,
would get a good education, no matter what sacrifices they
would have to make.

As I grew up they persistently drilled into me the idea that
all I must worry about was my school work. Therefore, my daily
dish was school, a little play and study. They, of course,
realized the need for recreation and play but wherever recreation and study conflicted, as they often did, study won out.
However in looking after my education they merely saw to it
that my school work was done and never sought to develop my
abilities along special lines, or to find out what abilities I
had. Thus when I now try to think of any special skills I possess I find it a very difficult task. In fact it is this question which is probably foremost in my mind at nearly all times.
I often think of what I can do in the future and find myself
puzzled and give up in despair.

At school, I found myself above the average but never among
the really smart fellows. Wherever I turned I would find others
better than I and would just let it go with the thought, "I
ain't so hot." However, I still feel that I would like to write
and that maybe some day in the future I will try it. Outside of
that small spark I never found anything I was skillful at in
school.

In the home I did very little, if anything and developed no
skill at doing little things as many young people do. I never
developed any athletic ability even though I enjoy sports a
great deal. This is probably due to the comparative lack of opportunity. However, I did find that when I started to participate in the dramatic activity of a club, I belong to that I was
enjoying it immensely and was fairly good at it in comparison
to some of the other members of the group. But of course when I
saw movies and plays I realized that I was really punk, but I
continue to do this type of work because of the enjoyment it

brings and because I wish to develop any little ability I may
have. I find that performing before people and getting their
applause makes me feel that I am really doing something. I feel
that as myself I couldn't make anybody feel my presence but
that when I act at least they are aware of me.

Outside of writing, acting and participating in sports as already mentioned, and adding reading, there is little I can think
of that I really enjoy, except such things as dancing and going
to the movies and plays. The notable absence is the lack of
something that might be an indication of my future vocation.

Reading is a great source of pleasure because, as has often
been said, it opens new worlds to me. It often serves as do the
movies a means of escape from everyday life. As far as sports
is concerned, it too serves as an escape. But this I don't believe is the important thing. Sports serves as an outlet for
the competitive urge in a form which is healthful and enjoyable
rather than destructive to others, as business competition, etc.
are. I feel when playing ball a thrill and feeling that I feel
in very few other things. I don't believe that I enjoy playing
because I can show my own ability, since there isn't much of
that, and since I enjoy myself even when losing.

II

For most of my life, I did not have much contact with other
kids. I had a very few friends and no intimate friends. This
was the beginning of a vicious circle. My lack of contact with
people led to fear on my part that I would not be able to get
along with other people. For this reason I kept even more to
myself, thus aggravating the situation. The one thing that
helped me was that I belonged to a children's club, that would
be considered "radical" by some. However it was only one night
a week, business was discussed and the meeting adjourned. Once
in a while we would have a party. It was here though that I met
the fellow who is now my only intimate friend.

I have always been the quiet type, being afraid of making a
bad impression by saying the wrong thing. I find that now,
though, I have come out of my shell quite a bit, I still am
afraid of that bogey "bad impression." I also find that as has
often been stated, I am friendly toward those who seem friendly
toward me. My ability to get along with people seems to have
improved since I was given the responsibility, at one time, in
my club, of speaking to new people. I have found thru my contact that people are very much like myself for a great part.
This knowledge, something I never seemed to realize before, has
given me great confidence.

Still the fact remains that I am somewhat backward. This is
especially true where girls are concerned. I never had much to

do with girls, having gone to an all boys high school and now
City College, and I am afraid that girls are even more particular, as far as fellows are concerned.

Since my club consists of people whose political ideas and
whose outlook on life are similar to mine, I feel more at home
with these people. It is from among them that my friends come
and they form practically my whole social life.

As far as people with whom I am intimate and those whom I dislike it seems a rather funny situation. I have always tried to
like people and make as few enemies as possible and yet I have
never wanted to become really intimate with people, perhaps
fearing that such intimacy might lead them to think me a funny
sort of guy and then have them "give me up."

I have but one intimate friend and another not quite so intimate but to whom I feel close. The former I met at the club
mentioned at first. Since that time we have been going practically everywhere together. It was not something that I chose to
do but something that came about unconsciously. We would play
together, go out together, and discuss our problems with each
other. This latter may be the important thing. I had never had
anybody I could confide in and he was a receptive audience and
in turn confided in me. Thus the bonds between us unconsciously
became stronger. The other friend is one whom I met at the college. We were in the same classes and lived in the same neighborhood. I used to travel home with him and discuss problems
together. He seemed intelligent and very friendly so I kept up
the association. After a while we used to go to each other's
houses, study together, and help each other out. Unfortunately,
he moved to another borough and contact is more difficult but
we still maintain very friendly relations.

As for whom I dislike. Well I couldn't name six but I can
give two offhand. One is a fellow somewhat older than myself
who is rather intelligent but who makes you know that he thinks
he is intelligent. There is continually an air of superiority
about him that I don't like. Another point against him is his
much too aggressive attitude towards girls. Perhaps it is jeal-
ousy but I think not. I have seen him acting somewhat intimately
with one girl one minute and a few seconds later doing the same
with another girl. He seems continually confident that sex ap-
peal simply oozes from him. Another fellow I dislike is a rather
rich kid I know, a little younger than myself, who makes himself universally disliked. He is afraid to let anybody play
with his ball for example. He too openly shows his dislikes for
people. At parties he acts like a baby, deriving lots of fun by
being filthy. In addition, he once told me that my best friend
was a "so and so" and didn't see why I even spoke to him. This

sneaky action does not make for any great love. His attempt to
buy friends by treating fellows to the movies, shóws, etc. put
him at the bottom of the heap as far as I was concerned.

As for people who are all right but whom I would not like to
know intimately, well I feel as before stated that I don't want
to have more intimate friends and have come to adopt the attitude that I'd like everybody for a friend but not as too close
a friend.

III

In my relations to those younger than I, I feel very comfortable. For a while I acted as a sort of "helper-out" to the
leader of a club of younger people and got along very well and
enjoyed doing the work. Helping younger fellows and girls gave
me some confidence and a feeling that I was really doing something. I find myself on excellent terms with my younger brother's friends and often play with them. In fact, I usually feel
more confident with them than with people of my own age.

I also get along fairly well with people older than myself.
The only hitch being with people who are much more intelligent
that I and whose discussions, beautiful way of speaking, and
general knowledge, make me feel pretty small. I find that in my
club those older than I accept me as one of them; however to
them age means little and since I have little contact with older
people outside the club I don't know how I could get along with
them. I consider myself an adolescent but really don't know of
any effect this has on my relations to others. It probably does
help me get along with those younger than I. Of course I feel
older when with these younger people but not old enough to make
any real difference.

IV

I feel "at home" mostly with people from my club, with whom I
have a lot in common but do not feel "at home" even with them
when I go to their houses or go out with them. I feel at home
mostly when with a crowd of young people. However, when with
young people, outside the club, who seem to think dancing, parties, and having a lot of fun is the most important thing, I
feel uncomfortable, mainly because I feel I can't live up to
their standards. I find myself in a corner, quiet, feeling con-
tent to let them get the laughs and being centers of attraction.

I rarely feel very confident of myself. Practically the only
time I am really confident is when with younger people where I
feel my superior knowledge and age command some respect. Since
I usually feel others are smarter than I or excel me in some
field I usually feel unconfident.

I seem continually plagued by a fear that I will never get
anywhere in life, that no job awaits me, and that I could do no

job really well. In fact this often leads me to feel that life
isn't worthwhile and consequently feel in a bad mood most of
the time. Of course my worries in school do a lot to keep me
down. I find myself always worried whether the problem warrants
it or not. I get along rather well in school getting only one
"D" and no flunks in two years of college work. Yet I seem
afraid that the tide will turn or something bad will happen,
Even while enjoying myself at parties or wherever it may be,
for seemingly no reason at all worries about the future interfere with school work.

VI

Due to the attitude written of above I find inner conflicts
between doing work and going out to have fun. There are times
however when I grit my teeth and say that if I'm going to have
any future I've got to study. Other times I think of what my
parents have done to keep me in school and say I can't let them
down, so I pitch in.

VII

Most of part seven can be answered by one thing. My dream of
heaven is not a heaven in the clouds but one here on earth (I
don't believe in the after life). I believe that there is
enough on this earth to satisfy the needs of all men. I believe
that our advancing industrial age can bring us all we want or
need. I think that with proper organization, this world could
be a heaven. There really is no need for people to find life a
dull routine of work, eat, and sleep, if you are lucky enough
to have a job. If instead of a system of capitalism, we had one
of socialism and eventually of communism, people would only
have to work six, later four hours a day as machines are developed and that the main things in life would be the pursuit of
what would bring the most happiness to the individual. Such a
world would equal any heaven that could be dreamed of. What is
more this is possible and will in the future be here. It is
while working to bring such a society closer that I find I am
happiest. If I had a magic wand I would wish that the people
would see this and bring it about. But as is often true if you
ask for a lot you get nothing. If I were to be more specific, I
would wish for a steady job at decent pay for myself, thus
eliminating one of my main worries.

The thought of my future and the thought of what is happening
in the world today are two sources of great unhappiness for me.
I have seen so much suffering, starvation, sickness, and read
so much of brutality, and war that it only makes me more determined that the cause of all this unhappiness must be eliminated.
If I had the ability, there is nothing I would rather devote my
life to than bringing about a better society.

VIII

Since most of my time is spent in school and most of the time
outside school is spent in doing school work, my main source of
anxiety is to get along well in school. As described before
this one is one of the main worries I have. Exams are the source
of tenseness and being upset for most students and so especially
at this time are for me.

IX

Due to my political ideas I find that people in one respect
fall into class categories. However I do not oppose or dislike
individuals because they are simply bourgeois or whatever it
may be. It seems clear to me that the basic organization of
life is economic. However, unlike those who misinterpret and
distort Marx, the economic bases for actions are realized not
to be the only ones. Social, religious, and political factors
are very important, but if we go back far enough we will find
that these latter factors are fundamentally economic. A change
in the economic system would change our social, religious, and
political set-ups. With this understanding I see things, people
in a certain light and consequently class them accordingly. I
look forward to the day when all men will be free really and
happy in a world of socialism.

Tolerance Analysis: Case #32

This subject presents a fairly consistent picture leading one
to expect of him a high degree of tolerance. He seems to have
been insulated from the common prejudices of the culture by
early membership in a "radical" group and apparently continuing
contact with it. Since he refers to it as a children's group,
we suspect his parents also of liberal leanings. Under the special circumstances he presents, it would not be necessary for
him to rebel against the mores of the majority to reject them:
he may never have been expected to accept them. Since on the
whole he seems a conforming sort of person, he may simply be
conforming to the tenets of a cultural subgroup which has been
more intimately his than what we usually think of as the dominant culture group. He states that he is an adherent of Marxist
doctrine, with profound faith in the economic basis for human
behavior. He would have to be equally accepting of all ethnic
groups to be self-consistent.

However, we have sometimes found subjects who were not altogether consistent, although they expressed similar political

leanings. These were moved by strong needs to reject or dominate others, not satisfied by the teachings of socialism. In
subject 32 we find some evidence for similar needs, but in his
case the aggressive impulses are turned against those who misinterpret Marx, and against causes of misery and suffering
rather than against individuals. He has passed sufficiently beyond the egocentric stage to be able to identify with others,
and to feel an essential kinship with them. His approach to individuals is generally positive, with no evidence of the projectivity that made some of our other subjects truculent and
suspicious. We find additional evidence for maturity in his
helpful attitude toward those who are younger than he and in
his eagerness to assume financial responsibility for himself.
Although he suffers keenly from feelings of inferiority, he
still feels capable of being socially useful.

On the whole, we have in #32 a fairly mature, fairly objective young person, who has found outlets for his dominance, aggression and recognition needs in dramatics and sports. Since
his accepted social philosophy prohibits the expression of
prejudice against ethnic groups per se, we find no indication
against a highly tolerant attitude.

Subject #28

I

I have acquired a great many skills. Most of these skills
have been learned outside of school and some of them have been
learned at the expense of my school work.

To enumerate them first I will take my avocational skills.
They are radio, photography, woodworking, metalcraft, machin-
ist's work, movie-making, and various games such as tennis,
miniature golf, handball, swimming, ping-pong, billiards, baseball and softball, skating, ice-skating, sleigh-riding, basketball and volley ball. My main vocational skill is in knowing
how to run a small grocery store. These classifications are not
necessarily rigid as I often made money from my hobbies. I will
explain this in the following paragraphs.

When I was a sophomore in high school, some of the fellows in
my neighborhood were radio operators. Listening to them talk
their lofty technical terms invested the profession with a certain glamour. Finding out that very little money was needed I
joined the school club and learned the fundamentals well. However in radio the monetary aspect of the situation grows as

your knowledge grows. This difficulty is overcome by the club
which is essentially a cooperative group pooling all resources.
About a year and a half ago, I was introduced into photography
in much the same manner. However I joined a well-knit, hard
working cooperative photographic group. Most of the people in
the group were older than I at the time. They ranged from doctors and school teachers to manual laborers. There was a spirit
of camaraderie that enabled one to become adjusted quickly to
the group. I took the elementary and advanced courses that the
club offered under capable teachers and in a year, thru intensive study and work that I enjoyed thoroughly, had become one
of the advanced members of the group. Photography is what I enjoy most but I cannot be classified as a rabid "candid camera
fan." Due to the high cultural level of the organization that I
joined, I view photography from a cultural viewpoint and do not
get inmeshed in a web of mechanical terms when I talk about
photography. Indeed, this is the difference between a good photography and a "candid camera maniac." One talks about prints,
their meanings, viewpoints and implication while the other
spouts technical terms at his poor listeners.

Before my father acquired his business, he was a carpenter
and I learned much about woodworking from him. I do not extensively practice carpentry but use it as the situation requires,
making an occasional bookcase, bench or toy.

My knowledge of metalcraft, that is, art metalcraft, came
thru a mutual interest in the subject on the part of my sisters
and myself. It is a hobby that I reserve for a rainy day when I
have no photography to do but my interest in it is kept up because of my sisters continual activity. I offer suggestions,
help out in small parts, but do not practice extensively.
Photography leads to an interest in movie making and I joined
the "Film and Sprocket Society" at the college. This is the
form that my extra-curricular activity in school takes and I
since have been elected an officer of the organization.

Most of the games I know I learned in school with the exception of handball, tennis, miniature golf, billiards, and ice-
skating. I enjoy playing all of these equally well and during
the summer when I have time for all, I rotate my activities, so
to speak.

My father is a small entrepreneur. He has a small store and a
moderate income and even though we came perilously near the
brink in 1929 we were never in need. However, there is another
aspect to the situation. The store is open from early morning
to well past midnight and requires the services of four people
to tend it. That is the green-eyed monster that spoiled a good
part of my youth. When other children were playing in the

street, a good part of my time was taken up learning prices,
taking my turn at the counter and helping the folks out around
the store in general. As a result of ten years of this I can
manage the store but there is no job that I hate more than the
drudgery of that store. This is reflected in our attitude toward the customers since we all have the same attitude. It is
not shown in surliness towards customers, but rather in the
cultivation of customers as friends rather than customers. Most
of our business is done leisurely and on a personal basis.

There are few things that I would like to do better to secure
more enjoyment. I would like to do more photography. If I only
had the time there are hundreds of things that I would like to
photograph and I look upon my friends with envy who go out to
shoot some pictures while I am fettered behind a counter.

II

My approach to my associates on the main is frank and open.
Of course, I take into consideration their various sensitivities
but this is not a fear on my part but rather a consideration
for them. Girls that I know well I consider on the same basis
as boys. However there is a reticence on my part to discuss matters of sex relations with girls who are comparatively strange
to me. There is no reticence such as this in my discussion with
boys of my own approximate age. The presence of an older man
however seems to silence any session on sex that the fellows
are having. My intimates are fellows of my own age with whom I
grew up and although I rarely see them now, this does not influence my attitude towards them. We all have political ideas
that are generally compatable. I find very little to dislike in
my intimates except one who is at times a braggart.

The following people affect me so that even being in the vi-
cinity makes me feel like going thru the mental torture of hell.
The first is a woman of about 35. She weighs about 250 pounds
and speaks like a two year old and has a terrible lisp to boot.
When she comes into the store, she slobbers over the food. She
babbles about pictures that she saw, hasn't got any real sense
of esthetic values and tells how this one made her cry and the
other made her laugh.

Until recently our apartment house had a Superintendent who
to the best of my knowledge never took a bath. Once when his
wife was in the hospital for two weeks during the summer, he
wore the same clothes for that time, because "I wouldn't touch
any woman's work." He was continually drunk and obnoxious in
his approach. On the basis of my being a tenant in his house,
he would clamp his hand on my shoulder and deluge me with his
barroom tales. I often wondered what motivated my landlord to
keep this individual the full six months that he was there.

A cigar salesman that walked into the store and proceeded to
make a target of a supposed high pressure sales talk and then
proceeded to regale me (he thought) with a few accounts of his
sexual exploits and some fatherly advice was a person I never
could stand. I simply refused to deal with him from then on and
let my father do all business.

A friend of mine has a girl friend who is so effusive and so
eager to please everyone that she simply gags me. I can't stand
the perpetual insistence of someone that I let them do something for me. I rarely see this friend now because he is usu-
with his girl friend and even when her attention is concentrated
on him I suffer.

I can't stand having anything to do with my F----- teacher,
yet I had to bear him all term. He would precipitate political
discussions on the benevolence of monarchies and dismiss all
arguments to the contrary with the statement "I am older than
you are, you don't know anything." My repugnance toward him is
due to continual aggravation without being able to state my
part.

A casual friend of mine is an electrical engineer. He seems
like a nice enough fellow but I wouldn't want to cultivate him
as an intimate because with what few experiences I had with him
I know that he would try to make me obligate myself to him. He
conveniently forgets debts and when he borrows anything it is a
tedious process to get it back. He is very voluble and when he
starts talking he doesn't stop for at least ten minutes. I know
that if I ever developed him as an intimate there would be no
end of tediousness for me.

I have a girl friend with whom I struck up a casual friendship and occasionally take out to dances. She seems like a nice,
ordinary pleasant girl but I found out that she was extremely
impatient and expressed no tolerance with the ideas of others.
I have ideas that clash with some of those of my intimates but
we respect each others ideas and do not evince an unpleasant
attitude.

A certain fellow that I know who indulges in sports occasionally with the fellows around the block finds his only enter-
tainment in the movies. Movies are the perpetual discussion on
his lips and he regards any other subject as topics that only
politicians, schoolmasters, and "foreigners" discuss. His
classification of "foreigner" annoys me. Anyone who argues with
him is a "God damned foreigner." I am sure he would indulge in
fisticuffs if anyone ventured to be so rash as to dislike a
movie that he liked and called him a foreigner.

III

I regard as culturally inferior those slightly younger than

myself and even of my own age when I came to college because
much of my culture had been gained from associations with people
ten to fifteen and even twenty-five years older than myself.
However, my attitude was modified considerably when I entered
college because I found I had been building a little cultural
world for myself mainly of restricted fields in music, art, and
science and that these other fellows and girls knew just as
much in different fields and that I could learn from them as
much as they could learn from me. Culturally I still associate
with people considerably older than myself, socially too, but I
reserve intimate associations for people of my own age. However,
I spent too much time in the world of the adult and used to
look down patronizingly at the doings of the adolescent. When I
look back and see what I missed I am keenly aware of a loss. I
feel the same both in the company of adults and adolescents.
This is probably due to the fact that most of the adults I associate with retain an informal youthful attitude even though
they are much older than I am. I feel old however when I see
young fellows and girls who I used to regard as babies growing
up and going out together and ask myself what I accomplished
while they were growing up.

IV

I feel at home first in my own home. I have a liberal family,
we all respect each other's ideas and all are mutually helpful.
There is no stern parent-child relationship but rather a spirit
of camaraderie. I also feel at home in the houses of my intimates. I know their folks well and do not have to be on guard
maintaining an air of proper etiquette. Then I feel at home
with people of the same cultural and political interests. I
talk these matters over freely with them and do not hold myself
back. I don't feel at home with strangers, persons with violently opposite political ideas, and persons who try to maintain an air of middle class respectability which is only a ve-
neer covering a host of actions that I dislike. A customer of
mine, a woman who I know of as a pinch penny in her dealings,
doesn't hesitate to cheat on her bill, but wears flashy clothes,
drives a car more or less skillfully, and looks down upon storekeepers and clerks with haughty disdain even though her husband
is only a small fur coat manufacturer who happened to hit the
jackpot by landing several large contracts. He has no illusions
as to his position but she certainly has. He is a well-mannered,
quiet person, well read, goes to concerts, appreciates different points of view and is generally well balanced.

V

I feel most confident in situations in which I take a thor-
ough knowledge of the matters at hand. I can make decisions

quickly in my job, or working at a hobby where a mistake would involve considerable time and expense. I feel least confident in situations in which I cannot understand the factors at hand and am worrying about the impression I am making on the people involved. When I sell portraits that I have taken I do not know what price to charge.

The fear that really disturbs me is the opportunity I will have of getting employment after school. I am afraid that the years spent in college acquiring a scientific knowledge will be wasted when I get a job doing clerical work in a broker's office or am stuck in a rut in my father's store. I am not denying the necessity for the cultural aspect but I worry as to whether I will be able to have my own home in the future with a certain amount of security.

VI

I have a terrific inner conflict when I have photographic work that must be done and I am scheduled to be in the store at the same time in order to relieve my father who has been on his feet since six in the morning till four in the afternoon. Most of the times I go to the store hoping for some future freedom but sometimes I call up, pretend an abundance of school library work and say I will not be home until late in the evening. I realize that it will give my father no end of discomfort and that he will be grouchy to the customers but I feel the need for a little recreation after school work when the tedium of the store would make me very irritable.

I also have an inner conflict when my small sister interrupts me in the midst of an intense period of work with a simple question. I feel like hitting her and starting a family row but usually hold back. Sometimes, I do hit her and immediately regret it because she bursts into tears at my seemingly unprovoked attitude and I realize the foolishness of my actions.

VII

I am happiest when I am doing something I enjoy thoroughly with the companionship of a person that I like very much. I can't conceive of stating what I would do with a magic wishing wand but I will give my conception of a perfect place to live in which amounts to using the wand.

In the perfect place to live in all men would work harmoniously at the tasks best-fitted for them, there would be food and clothing and desirable luxuries for all. Each would give according to his ability and receive according to his need. Students would concentrate on a study that they liked and there would be no compulsion for class attendance because they would attend out of sheer enjoyment. Disease would be reduced to a minimum that modern medical forces could attain. All work and

professions would be socialized so that the greatest common
good could be obtained.

There won't be any heaven for me because I don't believe in
supernatural powers. However, the ideal heaven would have my
mother and father waiting at the gates for me. There would be
eternal brotherly love among the denizens of the place and we
would all be intimate. I could get all the things I ever desired and could indulge in all those pleasures that I never had
time nor money for.

I am very unhappy when I see suffering either physical or
mental. Suffering profoundly distresses me and I do all in my
power to rectify it. I can't see how some people even maintain
a dispassionate attitude toward the wars in China and Spain today, ignore our social problems in their country such as the
slums and the sharecropper and completely tie themselves up in
a little world of their own.

VIII

I feel tense, anxious and upset when someone that I like is
very ill, or is in a perilous pecuniary situation. I also have
the same feeling when I try to make an impression on a girl
whose acquaintance I am particularly anxious of acquiring. A
certain tenseness pervades my being when someone who I particularly dislike strikes up a conversation with me. A certain
customer with whom I had a heated argument came back to the
store after an absence of three months. I ignored the previous
argument and treated him coldly and formally as though he was a
passerby who had entered to buy something. All during the time
that I was waiting on him I was particularly tense and con-
strained.

I felt distinctly uncomfortable recently when I walked into a
room after my mother had just finished lauding my capabilities
to a relative and was confronted with the necessity of showing
some marvelous portraits to her when all I had on hand were
some inferior practice shots. However she couldn't tell the
good from the bad and was mainly impressed by their size so
that everything turned out all right.

IX

For me the fundamental organization of life is that this
earth coupled with man's capabilities is capable of producing
enough so that one need not go ill fed and dressed and never
enjoy any cultural benefits. However the system under which we
live is organized in contradiction to this fundamental. Because
of the fact that there is so much, surpluses are destroyed or
curtailed and millions go needy.

I classify activities as cultural and vocational. The classifications are not rigidly but roughly. I would say that a man's

job is his vocation and his hobbies and pleasures constitute his culture.

I put people into three classes economically: workers, the middle class, and the capitalists. There is a continual struggle between the workers and the capitalists with the middle class being forced into the workers class by the capitalist or else outrightly supporting the capitalists. We speak of the great American middle class but I think this is a term that really gained pre-eminence because workers liked to be considered as respectable middle class.

Culturally I think we can make no such classification. With the medium of mass educational devices so prominent labor is. more and more getting its share of the culture that formerly belonged only to the aristocracy. Indeed if a classification is drawn, it is drawn from the fact that labor develops its own culture and we have prominent labor poets, artists, writers, and musicians.

People as individuals at first I classify according to physical attractiveness. However this classification really does not amount to much because my final analysis is on the basis of how much cultural rapport I can gain with them. I have friends who are truckdrivers, automechanics, machinists, schoolteachers, doctors, artists, storekeepers, musicians, writers, and photographers. If I can appreciate their point of view and can speak with them and partake with them on their cultural level everything is fine.

My worker friends, that is manual laborers and semi-skilled such as the truckdrivers and mechanics have a general awareness of the world situation. They are willing to discuss it, perhaps not in cultural terms, but from any angle quite realistically. They haven't the same cultural interests as I have but I can appreciate playing billiards, cards, and handball with them and they accept me as one of the fellows even though I go to college and use terms that occasionally they don't understand. My other friends have had much the same background as mine and I encounter no difficulty in getting along with them.

Tolerance Analysis: Case #28

This subject seems to be a comparatively mature, optimistic, energetic, socially outgoing person. His intimate family and social groups are characterized by liberal political tendencies. It is likely that during his formative years he was effectively prevented from acquiring the prejudices of the larger culture by the liberal leanings of his intimates. He rebels vigorously

against such prejudices, finding in this rebellion one outlet
for aggressive drives. His own accepted political and social
code expressly enjoins against discrimination on ethnic grounds,
and in an individual as well integrated as subject 28 seems to
be, we should expect a good deal of consistency in behavior. We
should, therefore, judge this subject to show a high degree of
tolerance with reference to ethnic groups.

When we review the emotional aspects of his personality, we
find no contra-indications to our first judgment. Strong aggressive drives are present, but are handled without resort to
repression or projectivity. The subject finds no difficulty in
expressing himself vigorously against "middle-class respectability," hypocrisy, persons with unpleasant mannerisms or physical characteristics, drudgery, suffering, and violence. He is
apparently aware of his own hostile reactions and handles them
on a conscious level. With many self-permitted channels for
draining off hostility, he does not have to bear the tensions
of repressed and denied negative feelings. He is free to make
social approaches on a realistic basis and to expend on others
a good deal of positive feeling. His positively toned experiences with people have cut across so many culturally delineated
boundaries that they have little personal meaning for him.

He has little trouble with feelings of inferiority, having
apparently a good deal of self-confidence and satisfaction in
his accomplishments. He has no need to compensate for a wilted
ego by proclaiming himself better than others by virtue of his
group membership. In short, he has no need to be intolerant or
derogatory of depersonalized ethnic groups, although he is frequently hostile towards individuals.

General Considerations

The presence of an organized intellectual code seems to be of
fundamental importance in the pictures of high tolerance. This
alone, however, is not decisive. There must be also the ability
to identify with others outside of the self and to handle frus-
trations and anxieties objectively. In addition, the capacity
for rebellion is involved, or enough fortitude to bear criticism. The resigned or fearful personality is generally conform-
ist..

It is assumed that a personal attitude of high tolerance is in contradiction to a general culture norm of low tolerance. We have seen a few cases, however, where such a personal attitude does not imply rebellion or lack of conformity. These subjects are simply conforming to a different set of tenets, to which they have been exposed during formative years by their families and intimate social groups. The capacity to rebel in these cases might result in rejection of family values and an apparent conformity to majority mores.

These observations suggest that further research might try to orient toward a study of the development of tolerance, not of intolerance. It might be fruitful to ask, "What are the factors that predispose an individual so that he develops a tolerant attitude?" rather than "What makes for intolerance?"

CHAPTER V

SALIENCE OF ETHNIC ATTRIBUTES

Description of the Attitude Variable: Salience

A PSYCHOLOGIST doing counselling at a Junior College in the New York metropolitan area reported the following.

A young man who had been coming for educational and vocational guidance was having trouble in his social relationships. His girl friend was Jewish and he was not. His friends were taking him to task for going out with the Jewish girl. "Tell me, Dr. E, is it true what they say about Jewish girls?" he blurted out one day. In the course of further discussion the counsellor asked, "You know that I am Jewish, don't you?" "Yes" the boy replied, "but I didn't think of it until after we had started speaking."

The tendency to be aware of the minority group membership of an individual may be considered a separate attitude variable for study. It may be studied in relation to tolerance and other factors in the discussion of race attitudes. In general, we may try to study the importance of the characteristic for the individuals serving as subjects in our research. This variable may be called the salience of the particular attitude. Stern discusses salience as the "embeddedness" continuum, the degree of prominence or emphasis which characterizes experience (16).

It may be quibbling but one might consider whether a psychologically sound analysis of the difference between attitudes of Germans towards Jews post- and pre-Hitler should not be largely in terms of the emphasis upon the dislike, not its degree. Jews were disliked in Germany for generations, Hitler brought this dislike to the foreground, gave it an emphasis it did not have formerly.

Erika Mann (8, page 54) points out that the schools of Nazi Germany set new fundamental maxims with a new scale of values.

The scale of values, in order of importance was set by the
Führer:

Hereditary tendencies; general racial picture.
The character (degree of adherence to National Socialism).
The physical makeup or "body" (degree of usefulness in the
event of a future war).
(And, last) Knowledge.

Whereas each of these values was represented in the school system before, to some degree, there is a new salience -- some
have increased in importance, others have decreased.

We might almost identify salience with a hierarchy of values,
and the measurement of the salience of a particular attitude
might be approached in a number of ways. The evidence for the
need for study of salience is not hard to find. LaPiere's study
of attitude expressed toward Chinese by hotel keepers and res-
tauranteurs and the lack of relation between the verbal expressions and the behavior in the situations where Chinese were
personally involved suggests that for complete description of
the relation of attitude to other behavior we must describe attitude more completely than by the customary schedule for degree of liking (7). Clyde Miller, in an analysis of employment
of teachers and administrators, lists eight items in the order
of importance (10). They are (1) supply and demand, (2) education and preparation, (3) experience, (4) personality and character, (5) intelligence, (6) health, (7) prejudice and favoritism, (8) luck or chance. In the discussion of prejudice and
favoritism, we learn that

...prejudice and favoritism are most pronounced in times of
economic and political stress. There are prejudices for and
against persons on the basis of age, sex, race, marital status, religion. Irrespective of proved fitness, candidates
often fail to obtain positions because of these things.

In the discussion of the list as a whole, it is pointed out
that these eight items are listed in the approximate order of
importance. We also learn that

...largely beyond his control also are the forces of emotion found in the factor of Prejudice and Favoritism; and the caprice which enters into the play of Luck or Chance. Even the basic factor of Supply and Demand may be set aside by Prejudice, Favoritism, Luck or Chance.

Apparently there is not only variation in the degree of prejudice as an abstracted attitude, we may also expect to find the importance of the prejudice varying as a function of factors unrelated to the prejudice itself.

Approach to Salience Measurement on Sociological Level

In the Gestalt theory of personality, in Stern's personalistic approach, in G. W. Allport's attempt at clarification, we find an emphasis on the need for understanding those factors within the individual which represent the most salient aspects of the personality. If our interest is in the study of an attitude or attitudes, we must find some method for objective description of the salience of the attitude.

One approach which seems a useful starting point is the relative frequency that a given variable is mentioned under controlled conditions. The classified advertisement section of the NEW YORK TIMES was chosen for preliminary review. The first Sunday in each of the months of January, April, July, and October, for the years 1930 to 1939, were selected. The total number of advertisements in the appropriate classification was tabulated, and within that total number, a tally was made of the frequency of those which made some direct reference to race, nationality, or religion. The research findings reported in the earlier chapters seem to demonstrate the generalized nature of certain aspects of intolerance and it was decided at this point not to classify separately the different forms of reference. Every reference was counted. Thus an employer who asked applicants to "write stating age, education, experience and religion" was tallied along with the person who might advertise: wanted-- "Cook, white," or wanted--"Nurse, English," as all were considered ethnic references. Ethnic references expressed as a percent of the number of advertisements within the classification, analyzed separately by sex, type of work, and whether the advertisement was help wanted or job wanted, are presented graphically in Figures 7A, B, C, and D.

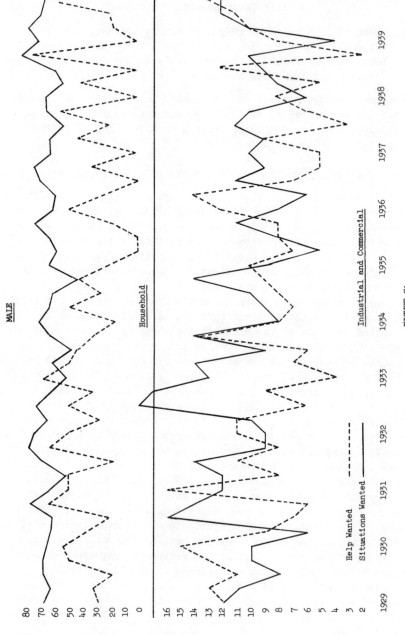

MALE

Household

Industrial and Commercial

Help Wanted ----------
Situations Wanted ————

1929 1930 1931 1932 1933 1934 1935 1936 1937 1938 1939

80
70
60
50
40
30
20
10
0

16
15
14
13
12
11
10
9
8
7
6
5
4
3
2

FIGURE 7A

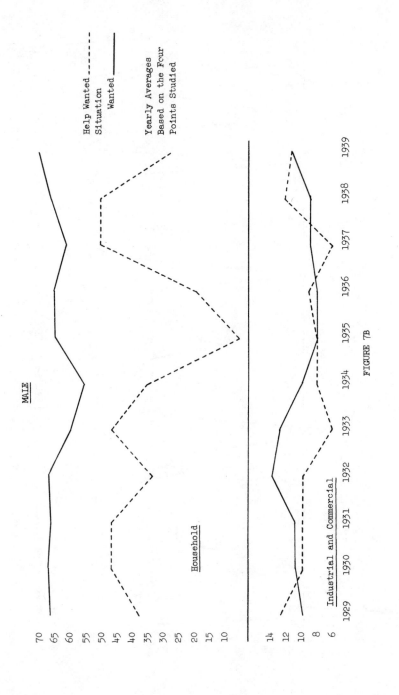

FIGURE 7B

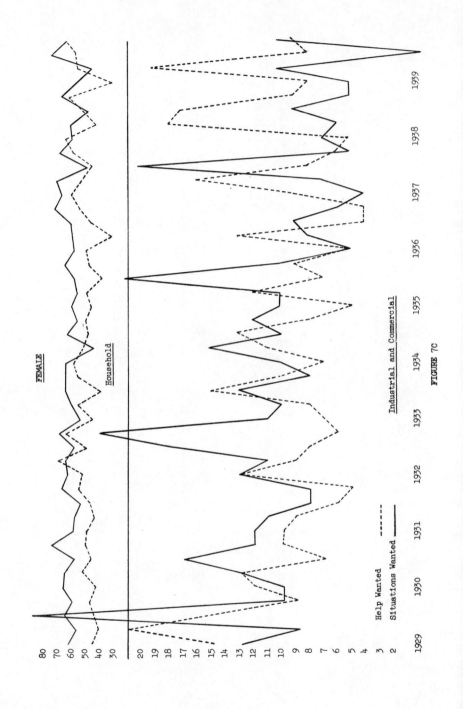

FEMALE

Household

Industrial and Commercial

Help Wanted ------
Situations Wanted ———

FIGURE 7C

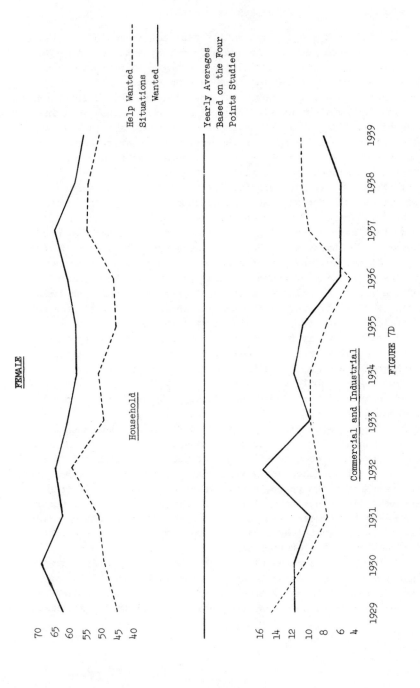

FEMALE

Help Wanted -------
Situations
Wanted ———

Yearly Averages
Based on the Four
Points Studied

Household

Commercial and Industrial

FIGURE 7D

From the analyses we may readily see that there is far greater
ethnic salience relevant to domestic employment than there is
for commercial and industrial jobs. Among male domestic workers
there is greater ethnic salience than among their prospective
employers. This relationship is less clear in the advertisements
of and for females, and is obscured in the commercial and industrial realms. We might be inclined to postulate that with
greater personal intimacy in the work relationship there tends
to be a greater amount of ethnic salience, but Figure 8 suggests
that it is necessary to qualify such a conclusion.

In Figure 8, we find graphically presented the proportion of
advertisements for apartments and rooms to share which make an
ethnic reference. Sharing an apartment seems fully as intimate
a contact as one involving domestic service, yet the former
seems to fluctuate about 20 percent and the latter about 50 percent. It may well be that the principle governing ethnic salience and intimacy of contact would apply within the framework
of the employer-employee relationship, but that once the framework of equality such as is employed in the sharing of an apartment is functioning, the salience will automatically be less-
ened, though it may be greater in the sharing of an apartment
with an equal than in club membership or school association
with social equals. The differences between employer and employee suggest that salience might be studied in relation to
the specific status of the individual, but for the present no
statement of "laws" will be attempted.

The figures show the points plotted for each tabulation computed. Summary figures, recapitulating the material in terms of
annual averages weighted for each of the four months according
to the relative number of advertisements, show more clearly the
trends through the years, minimizing the seasonal variations.
Seasonal variations occur most obviously with respect to advertisements for summer camp jobs. There are probably other factors
which are somewhat less obvious. A more careful analysis does
not seem warranted at this time. It is interesting to note that
there is no marked regularity of the change in relative frequency with which race references are made in the categories
investigated. This holds true for all classes of advertisements
except apartments to share. The general observation that there

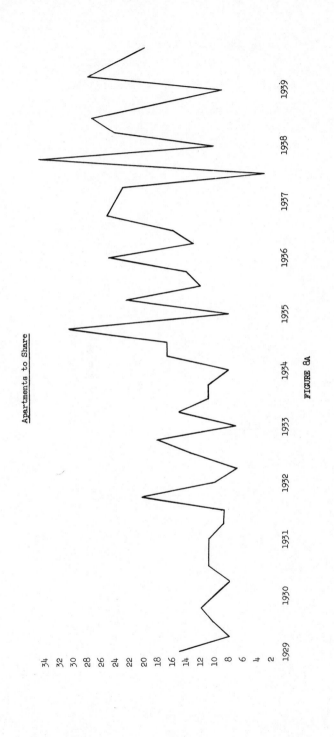

Apartments to Share

FIGURE 8A

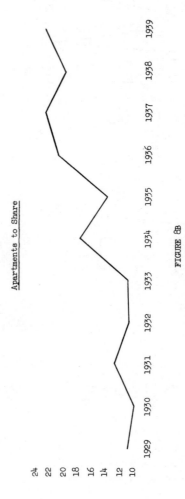

Apartments to Share

FIGURE 8B

Yearly Averages for the Four Points Studied

is an increasing emphasis on ethnic factors may not be adequately tested by these data, for the grographical segment sampled cannot be considered representative of the country, and the data selected for analysis may already have reached their maximum. Presumably, job-getting activities and employment relationships are very sensitive indices of small quantities of prejudice, and once the minimum is past may no longer be sensitive to variation.

The analysis here has been very crude. No differentiation was made between different types of ethnic characterization. In practice, we must recognize that an advertiser might request an English governess because of the high prestige factors attached to that national background. Another advertiser might solicit a Negro cook because of the economic cheapness and general inferiority characterization of that racial designation. This material is not always an index of prejudice against a group. It is, rather, relevant to a study of the consideration given to the factor in employment opportunities. Much more research should be undertaken in order to clarify the real issues involved. For the purposes of the present study it seems sufficient merely to call attention to the operation of this factor in the general social milieu.

Salience as a Psychological Variable

In this study, we are particularly interested in ethnic salience and the individual. The personality outline described in Chapter IV gives ample opportunity for subjects to express themselves relatively freely concerning the important variables which characterized for them different individuals and different situations. The final question, in fact, asked for a specific scheme for the classification of people. Sample responses by the students show that people were classified according to:

Age and sex.
The intelligent, the dull, the educated, the uneducated, the rich, the poor, the good looking, the ugly, the backward, the shining personality.
I have not seen a fair sample of the types of the human race to be able to classify them into categories. When I

do this I am trespassing in rather unsure territory. I
have known only neurotics intimately enough to classify
them and I do not wish to have this tinge in my general
classification of humanity.
Those whom I want to associate with those whom I don't
like.
I place them on two sets of teams. One...is the Spanish
Athletes (bull-throwers) versus the truthful and sincere
people. The second team consists of those who do evil to
other people versus those who fight them on the side of
law and those who do not hurt other people by their method
of living.
Due to my political ideas I find that people...fall into
class categories.

We also find classifications "according to wealth, religion and
nationality," and "the very poor, the poor worker, the moder-
ately wealthy, the rich. From another point of view I see the
dull, the students and the well educated. In religion, I see
the atheists, the Sunday churchgoer, and the zealous follower."
  A tally of the frequency with which individuals made ethnic
references during the course of filling out the entire outline,
based on forty-seven cases collected from C.C.N.Y.--Arts students, yielded the results indicated in Table XV.

TABLE XV

Frequency Distribution of Ethnic References in
Filling Out Personality Outline

Frequency of References	N
0	20
1, 2	15
3, 4, 5	7
6, 7, 8	2
9 - 14	1
15	2
	47

Of the forty-seven cases, twenty found no occasion to make any ethnic reference at all. Two included fifteen such references. The salience of ethnic characteristics for these two might legitimately be inferred to be far greater than for the twenty. It would seem unwise to generalize from these data drawn from only one sample of college students to college students in general. This particular group of students is drawn from a metropolitan center, is comparatively tolerant and is composed of generally discriminated against minorities. At other institutions we should not be surprised to find many fewer students making no ethnic references. We cannot elaborate the differences to be expected at this time.

Another approach to the measurement of salience was made. A set of photographs of boys and girls of college age were collected and mounted upon cards. The pack was then given to individuals during the course of individual testing in a series of exploratory studies, with the directions to "sort them out into piles. You can make as many piles as you want to or as few as you want. You can put as many into a pile as you want to or as few as you may choose. You can classify them on any basis you want to." After the first sorting the different piles were separately reviewed by the subjects and resorted. A third subdivision was attempted. Then they were all shuffled together again and another classification scheme was made. Further experimentation was done, calling for ratings in terms of general liking for the individuals' pictures and some studies with named faces.

This approach proved interesting on an individual basis. There were those boys who could subdivide the girls' pictures into five or six classification schemes, but put all the boys together into one category. Other boys could subdivide the group of boys, but the girls represented a unitary classification. For some, sex was disregarded and people were sorted on the basis of other characteristics, boys and girls being put into the same classifications without distinction. One individual was very careful to segregate those who wore glasses from those who did not, and confessed later that he had but just begun to wear glasses himself and was very conscious of them.

Another individual sorted the cards on a basis of the numeri-

cal quality of the identification numbers, first sorting on the
basis of odds and evens, then as multiples of 3, 5, and 7. This
individual had come to the clinic for consultation because of
his inability to make any sort of social contact. After he was
examined with the picture sorting test he was asked to write
out a description of his best friend. Analysis of this description showed a very similar approach. The friend was described
in terms of height, weight, complexion, college courses taken,
with absolutely no approach to any of the more subtle aspects
of the friend's personality, and without the slightest personal
evaluation. Descriptions of the two next best friends showed a
similar type of objectivity in approach. (It might be interesting to note that suggestions made concerning the possibility of
sensitivity to personal qualities practiced first on the pictures, and then in descriptions of classmates were later reported by the subject to have been helpful in improving his social relationships.)

The validity of the technique as an approach to understanding
the social orientation of the individual seemed clinically justified. The responses could be classified* as (1) objective
non-social, e.g. looking to the right, looking to the left; or
hair parted on the side, in the middle, or not at all; high
forehead, round face or oval face. (2) objective-social, e.g.
intelligence, active, energetic. (3) subjective social, e.g.
people I like, people who would be fun to go out with, people I
don't like. Those who tended to classify the photographs in the
latter scheme seemed better adjusted socially than those who
used the first system.

This test, while helpful in the clinical analysis of individuals and a promising device for further development, required
individual administration and was modified for purposes of the
present study. A "Faces Test," to be described in detail below,
was the finally standardized adaptation for use in the present
investigation for group administration.

---

*This is offered very tentatively as a suggestion for further
research. It is based on simple impressionistic study. Much
more extensive analysis will be needed before the technique can
be considered standardized.

Pictures of twenty-four seniors were selected at random from the annual publication of a metropolitan college. These students had all graduated several years prior to the beginning of the present study. In the series of questions asked about these "stimuli," three were designed to lend themselves to qualitative analysis. Questions 6, 7, and 8 of this "Faces Test" called for the specific description of three of the individuals pictured. In question 6 the directions were, "Look at individual Number 2. What sort of a person is this individual? Describe Number 2, in the space below, putting down the elements in your description just as they occur to you. Do not try to organize a theme. Number each item, in order, as you write it down." Directions for question 7 were, "Write ten (10) things you can say about Number 8. Number the items." Question No. 8 had as its direction "What can you say about Number 13?" The individuals responding to the test were permitted to put down whatever they felt they could say about the pictured people, relying entirely upon their own orientation, the way in which they regarded individuals. This test was administered to 140 students at C.C.N.Y.--Business and the analyses below refer to this sample.

Preliminary general analysis of the responses from eighteen men to question No. 7 -- "Write ten (10) things you can say about Number 8. Number the items" -- offers some orientation to the general trend of the responses. Not all of the eighteen subjects were able to give ten statements. A total of only 140 items was given (instead of 180). These descriptions were studied as a unit. They seemed to fall into the following organization with the proportion of the ratings classified in each group indicated as a percent of the total.

1. General Comment 5%
2. General Appearance 8%
3. Physical Appearance 5%
4. Total Personality 5%
5. Mentality 14%
6. Specific Personality Traits 36%
7. Interests and Work Habits 11%
8. Sociability 16%
9. Background (the race concept is included here) 2%

Ethnic references were only part of the "background" classification. Other references to family were included. Apparently
fewer than 2 percent of the items used to describe picture No.8
referred to ethnic characteristics as here discussed.

The further analysis of the salience factor proceeded in terms
of study of the tendency on the part of individual respondents
to use an ethnic reference. In describing three individuals,
the respondents might be expected to use an ethnic reference
with respect to each of the three, two of the three, one of the
three, or none of the three. Table XVI presents a frequency distribution of the students in terms of the frequency with which
they made ethnic reference in their description of the three
faces. It will be noted that 78.6 percent of the sample made no
reference to ethnic background while 21.4 percent, in their
spontaneous descriptions, mentioned this feature one, two or
three times. How are we to consider these references?

TABLE XVI

*Frequency of References to Ethnic Background in Describing
Three Pictured Individuals Made by Students in One Sample*

Frequency of References	Number of Students	Percentage
0	110	78.6
1	21	15.0
2	7	5.0
3	2	1.4
Total	140	100.0

If we assume that ethnic reference to a person is a relatively
chance phenomenon from the point of view of the psychology of
the person making such references, we might expect its occurrence in successive descriptions to be "independent" events. If
we estimate the probability of its occurrence in terms of its
obtained frequency of occurence in the sample, we find $p = 41/420$
$= .098$. (In describing each of three portraits, 140 subjects prepared a total of 420 descriptions. Of the 420 descriptions, 41

included estimates of the ethnic background of the individual described.) We can apply the probability theory to the problem of the frequency of occurrence of independent events where p=.098, and considering frequencies of occurrence in 140 combinations of three descriptions. The result of such an analysis is presented in Table XVII. Comparing the observed frequencies with the frequencies computed based on the hypothesis that successive descriptions of the pictures are "independent" events, each with probability of occurring as actually observed in the sample (p=.098) using the chi-square test, we find $\chi^2=35.1903$. With n=3, this chi-square value shows that the probability of finding such divergence on the basis of random sampling errors is less than .01 and that we may interpret the difference between the obtained distribution and that based upon such an assumption to be truly significant.

TABLE XVII

Expected Frequency of Occurrence of the Different Combinations of Ethnic Reference on the Hypothesis that the Descriptions Represent "Independent" Events

No. of References	Expected Frequency	Observed Frequency
0	102.74	110
1	33.49	21
2	3.64	7
3	.13	2
	140.00	140

The discussion to this point would seem to demonstrate that making ethnic reference in the description of a series of individuals represents a function which is not a chance or random performance. One point of question remains in consideration of the statistical analysis undertaken. We have assumed that the probability of making ethnic reference in the description of each picture is equal. More careful analysis does not confirm this assumption. The proportion of responses making ethnic reference in describing picture 6 was .07; picture 7, .15; and picture 8, .06. These differences suggest that there may be individual differences in the stimulus value of different pictures as determinants of ethnic reference in description.

A more direct test of the independence of the tendency to make ethnic references on successive descriptions was undertaken in a final and crucial form. The responses to the individual items were successively paired and chi-square test of the independence of the responses was made. The results of these tests are presented in Table XVIII. Here we find the evidence to indicate conclusively that the successive responses are not independent, that there is a distinct tendency for an individual making no ethnic reference in one description to make none in another, and for an individual who does make one ethnic reference to make another. The tendency to make ethnic reference is therefore to be considered a characteristic of the responding individual.

TABLE XVIII

Direct Test of Independence of Tendency to Make Ethnic References on Successive Characterizations. Chi-Square Test of Paired Responses

Paired Items	χ^2	n	P
6, 7	16.9	1	< .01
6, 8	13.4	1	< .01
7, 8	7.44	1	< .01

The tendency to use an ethnic reference is distinctly not a chance phenomenon. Our discussions and tests above indicate that any effort to describe the responses of the students as being haphazardly presented fails. Study of the comparisons in Table XVII shows that the chi-square value comes largely from those people who tend to make some ethnic reference. There is a surplus of individuals in the observed distribution over the theoretical distribution in those cells containing no reference and two and three references. The cell of one reference in the observed distribution has fewer cases than the corresponding frequency in the theoretical distribution. Apparently there is evidence for a tendency either to use ethnic reference or not use such reference, and this tendency is a distinct psychological entity, an entity which merits further study.

Some Concomitants of Ethnic Salience

On the basis of the data already available from the preceding series of studies, some preliminary efforts were made to analyze the factors related to the presence of ethnic salience in the individual. For an index of salience the Faces Test, as a whole, was used. In questions 2 and 3, the test respondents were asked to classify the pictured individuals in accordance with some scheme which they chose to create. It is possible to make ethnic references in a classification scheme. Items 6, 7, and 8, discussed above in detail, are the descriptions of three of the pictured individuals, and here there are three more chances for displaying salience. Item 10 calls for the definition of what the respondent thinks is his "kind of people." Here again there is a possibility for making or not making an ethnic reference. These items permit scoring from zero references to six. The 140 cases were divided into two categories: Those who made no reference and those who made one or more ethnic references. The distributions of these two categories on the variety of traits and test scores for which data were available were made and chisquare test applied to estimate the probability that divergence in the distributions represent only the sort of differences that might be expected on the basis of random sampling.

Perhaps of greatest interest in the present study was the test of relationship between ethnic salience and general tolerance towards nations and races. The differences that obtained between those who displayed some salience and those who showed none seem on the borderline of significance, $p = .05 > .10$. While not sufficiently great to warrant finality, it certainly does not preclude the possibility of there being a real difference. It was interesting to note that in this sample those with salience were more tolerant than those without.

Of more clear cut significance, p=.01 < .001, is the relationship between salience and sociality as described in item four of
the Faces Test. This item asks the subjects to indicate those of
the pictured individuals with whom they thought they might be
able to develop a close friendship. It was scored simply in terms
of the number of individuals the respondents encircled. This
index of sociality is, then, on a relatively "unreal" level.
This analysis suggests that those displaying ethnic salience
show significantly less sociality on the item than those without.

No significant relationships were found between the salience
feature and either of the two Flanagan scale scores of the
Bernreuter test.

To summarize this chapter, an attempt has been made to conceive the attitude variable of <u>salience</u> in a fashion which permits its quantification. We may study salience in either of two
general connotations. One, what may be the most salient things
for the subject in a standardized situation? This approach gives
interesting clues to the study of personality of individuals. A
second approach involves a specific attitude variable; when we
are concerned with the study of a particular attitude in a standardized situation, how strong is the tendency for this aspect
of the situation to occur within the individual? This second
phase of the study of salience was undertaken with respect to
ethnic attitudes. A general approach to its measurement on a sociological level has been indicated and demonstration analyses
prepared. Further study of this factor as a variable related to
the behavior of the individual was made. These analyses demonstrated that we may consider the tendency to make ethnic references a psychological characteristic of the respondent. Individual differences in ethnic salience appear. Variability in ethnic
salience does not seem to be clearly correlated with tolerance.
A significant relationship was found between presence of ethnic
salience and constriction of the sociality of the individual.
(Another significant relationship was demonstrated between the
presence of ethnic salience and lack of confidence in the fair-
ness with which society rewards ability with success.*) The
findings reported in these analyses must be limited by consideration of the nature of the sample on which they are based.

*To be reported elsewhere.

CHAPTER VI

A SUMMARY OF THE STUDIES

IT IS VERY UNLIKELY that attitude toward a single group represents a unitary characteristic within the individual holding
the attitude. Not only is there difference within attitude toward Jews which separates European Jews from American Jews,
Jews in general and Jews you know, the corner grocer and Albert
Einstein, but there are the general attitudes of right and
wrong, attitudes concerning personal relationships, employer-
employee relationships, and so on, which influence the social
expressions of an individual in this realm. This point of view
can be supported not only by generalization of psychological
theory based on empirical study; but by studies such as those
of Minard (11), LaPiere (7), and Horowitz (6) on race attitudes.
Considerable study still needs to be done concerning the psychological organization of the individual and the nature of attitudes.

For purposes of the present study, a single realm of inquiry
was defined and questionnaire approach was made to college students. Within the framework of the questionnaire, prejudices
could be displayed toward several different ethnic groups. Within this framework it was found that tolerance-intolerance toward these ethnic groups represented a fairly generalized unitary function. Though we cannot predict from this particular
framework to others, the evidence suggests that within a defined framework we may expect intolerance of some one group to
be accompanied by intolerance of others, and relative tolerance
of one group to be accompanied by tolerance of others. The general tolerance-intolerance function is unitary and its degree
varies from individual to individual, and from group to group.
The generalized nature of this attitude was sufficient to cause
relatively high correlation between expressions of attitude toward existing groups and toward non-existing groups. This correlation was sufficiently high and sufficiently prevalent among
the widely different samples studied to suggest that in order

to understand attitudes toward a particular group we must first
have more insight into the generalized tolerance attitudes. We
might almost consider the attitude expressed toward some one
group a particularization, a differentiation out from this generalized approach to peoples. Analysis of the details related to
the response of an individual towards any one group would probably be obscured by the many individual and "chance" determinants. Our approach to the generalized tolerance seemed more
likely to lead us along the trail of a psychological fundamental.

In addition to the generalized intolerance-tolerance function,
more careful examination revealed a patterning of preference
for different ethnic groups which was uniform throughout the
samples studied. This pattern was not related to the actual contact an individual may have had with the members of the groups
included in the pattern, but seemed to represent part of the
general United States culture pattern. This hierarchy of preferences is relatively constant and is to be found among practically all sections of the populations; its roots spread down-
ward through the age scale, manifesting itself even among relatively young children. This pattern is based upon the historical
background of our country, its original settlers and later im-
migrants. This pattern is illustrated in a codified form in our
present immigration restrictions.

Members of minority groups that rank relatively low in the
heirarchy tend to incorporate the prevailing pattern as a whole
into their value system, with the unique exception of their own
group. "Own group" is placed at the top of the list and the
rest of the pattern tends to remain intact. Concrete experience
with the members of the groups in the hierarchy may cause minor
variation in the pattern of preferences, but the effect of such
experience must be considered a decidedly unimportant factor
when considering race prejudice as it is manifested on the con-
temporary social scene. Preferences are built up and attitudes
towards groups are developed relatively independently of personal contact with the group in question or its members.

Although the pattern of preferences is predetermined in this
country, there are distinct differences between the levels of
tolerance within which this pattern is ordered. Tolerance for
nations and races may be considered with reference to some arbi-

trary social scheme for evaluation. When studied in this fashion, groups are found to vary greatly in the level of tolerance
which might be used to describe their responses to ethnic groups
in spite of the fact that hierarchies of preferences are the
same. Thus, we found that students at one school, ranking Jews
toward the bottom of their schedule of preferences, were objectively responding toward this religious minority more favorably
than the students of another school were responding toward Danes,
though in the latter school Danes ranked toward the top of the
list of preferences. These differences in the levels of tolerance manifested by groups were observed in the present study,
but it was not deemed feasible to pursue the analysis of the
factors determining such group differences on the basis of college samples available. It did seem feasible, however, to attempt to explore factors associated with individual differences.

To what is the generalized tolerance level related? First, it
must be remembered that it is determined by those general laws
which govern the differences among groups. With reference to individuals, Murphy and Likert studied generalized tolerance and
demonstrated that it is positively correlated with higher grades
in courses in college. They showed it to be correlated positively with the tendency toward "dissatisfaction" with some
relatively general aspects of the American scene. Also it is
positively correlated with a tendency toward "radicalism" as defined in their study. These three general findings were reported
on the basis of independent analyses of students at the University of Michigan and Columbia University (12).

From the present study, we note that individuals who consider
members of different national and religious groups similar tend
toward tolerance. Individuals with more flexibility in regard to
ways of doing things may be more tolerant. College students, with
relatively good parental relationships appear more tolerant.
These suggestions are very tentatively offered, with no implications of causality involved. They seem sufficiently fruitful to
warrant presentation, though it is recognized that the correlations on which they are based are too low to justify generalization.

When the problem of individual differences was approached with
the methodology of clinical analysis, constellations emerged of
the generally tolerant and the generally intolerant personalities within the sample selected for such study.

The relatively tolerant personality seemed likely to exhibit
some combination of the following characteristics: a strong desire for personal autonomy, associated with a lack of need for
dominance; a strong need for friendliness, along with a personal seclusiveness, fear of competition; a tendency to placate
others along with lack of general conformity to the culturally
dominant mores. He appeared to be fairly serious, to be interested in current events, to have ideas about bettering society,
to be a member of a political group and to have great need for
personal achievement in the vocational area. He showed himself
to be an accepting personality, disliking violence, able to appreciate the contributions of others, conscious of feeling that
people tend to be more or less alike and adopting a nurturant
rather than a dominant attitude toward those younger than he.
He manifested conscious conflicts concerning loyalties and duties and was very seriously concerned about moral questions.
His interests centered about what are commonly called the social
studies, and about reading and journalism. Although personally
seclusive, he showed great need to be socially useful.

The relatively intolerant personality was found to combine in
varying degrees the following characteristics: unwillingness to
accept responsibility; acceptance of conventional mores; a rejection of serious groups; rejection of political interests,
and desire for groups formed for purely social purposes and absorption with pleasure activities; a conscious conflict between
play and work; emotionality rather than rationality; extreme
egocentrism; interest in physical activity, the body, health.
He was likely to dislike agitators, radicals, pessimists. He
was relatively uncreative, apparently unable to deal with anxieties except by fleeing from them. Often his physical activity
had in it a compulsive component. (It may be that this compulsion to be on the move, that is, constantly occupied with
sports, motoring, traveling, etc. served for him the same function as did study and activities with social significance for
the individual with high tolerance.)

In evaluating the summaries of the personality characteristics
of the tolerant and intolerant individuals, it must be remembered that these students were selected as extremes within a
group which is not particularly representative either of the

general population or, for that matter, of "typical college
students." There is no particular reason to believe without
evidence that the results do not apply to others, but until
evidence is produced we must be very careful about extending
these findings beyond the sample studied. Attention should be
called, too, to the fact that we are referring here to the generalized tolerance function, not to the specific attitude toward any one group.

Though many studies of actual abilities and potentialities of
different racial, national and religious groups have demonstrated that there are no necessary generalizations concerning
individuals which can be made solely on the basis of the ethnic
group background of an individual, nevertheless, judgments are
made in terms of ethnic background in a variety of situations.
The tendency to emphasize ethnic group affiliation was investigated in the present study and discussed as a definite attitude
variable. This variable is designated "salience." An approach
to its measurement on a sociological level was indicated and
demonstrated analyses prepared. Further study of this factor as
a variable related to the behavior of the individual was made.
These analyses demonstrated that we may consider the tendency
to make ethnic references a psychological characteristic of the
respondent. Individual differences in ethnic salience were evident. Variability in ethnic salience did not seem to be clearly
correlated with tolerance. A significant relationship was found
in a limited sample between presence of ethnic salience and re-
striction of the outgoingness of the individual.

While every effort was made to conduct the study in such fashion that the results might be applied to other samples of the
general population, we must again call attention to the fact
that most of the studies of the personality correlates of the
attitudes of tolerance-intolerance were made on students representing one type of community. Only further study can determine
the limitations which must be imposed upon our findings as a
result of this selection. Meanwhile, we may accept them as a
possible orientation for consideration of the general community
and we can consider them, to the extent that the statistical
evaluation permits, as representative of at least one segment
of the community.

APPENDIX TABLE A

*Date of Administration of Attitude Tests at the Different
Colleges and Whether Signatures Were Elicited*

Name of School	Date Given	Signature
"A" - Teachers College	Dec. 14, 1938	Optional
Bennington College	Dec. 20, 1938	Signed
College of the City of New York, Arts. (1st test*)	Dec. 9, 1938	Signed
College of the City of New York, Business	March 1, 1939	Signed
Columbia	Nov. 30, 1938	Signed
Howard	Dec. 21, 1938	Optional
"B" - Normal School	Dec. 16, 1938	Optional
Princeton	March 22, 1939	Optional

*Re-test, Jan. 6, 1939 - Signed.

BIBLIOGRAPHY

1. Bogardus, E. S. "A Social Distance Scale," Sociology-Social Research, XVII (1933) 265-271.
2. Bogardus, E. S. Immigration and Race Attitudes. Boston: Heath, 1928.
3. Chesire, L., Saffir, M., Thurstone, L. L. Computing Diagrams for the Tetrachoric Correlation Coefficient. Chicago: University of Chicago Bookstore, 1933.
4. Flanagan, J. C. Factor Analysis in the Study of Personality. Stanford University: Stanford.University Press, 1935.
5. Guilford, J. P. "Racial Preference of a Thousand American University Students," Journal of Social Psychology, II (1931) 179-204.
6. Horowitz, E. L. "The Development of Attitude toward the Negro," Archives of Psychology, XXVIII, No. 194 (1936).
7. LaPiere, R. T. "Attitudes vs. Actions," Social Forces, XIII (1934) 230-237.
8. Mann, E. School for Barbarians. New York: Modern Age Books, 1938.
9. Meltzer, H. "Group Differences in Nationality and Race Preferences of Children," Sociometry, II (1939) 86-105.
10. Miller, C. R. "Eight Factors in Employment," Section II in (Anon.) Employment of Teachers and Administrators. New York: Bureau of Educational Service of Teachers College, Columbia University.
11. Minard, R. D. "Race Attitudes of Iowa Children," University of Iowa Studies in Character, IV, No. 2 (1931).
12. Murphy, G. and Likert, R. Public Opinion and the Individual. New York: Harper and Brothers, 1938.
13. Murray, H. A. et al. Explorations in Personality; a Clinical and Experimental Study of Fifty Men of College Age. New York: Oxford University Press, 1938.
14. Rice, S. A. "Stereotypes: a Source of Errors in Judging Human Character," Journal of Personnel Research, V (1926-1927) 267-276.

15. Sherif, M. The Psychology of Social Norms. New York: Harper and Brothers, 1936.
16. Stern, W. General Psychology from the Personalistic Standpoint. New York: The Macmillan Co., 1938.